"Using evidence from internationally known and appreciated poets and writers, Richard Trim offers a novel and powerful account of how figurative language, especially metaphor, emerges in literary texts. The 6-step process he outlines is the most complete investigation to date of the issue of why and how authors use particular metaphors in their works".

Professor Zoltán Kövecses, Loránd Eötvös University, Budapest, Hungary

Mapping the Origins of Figurative Language in Comparative Literature

This book investigates the origins of figurative language in literary discourse within a cognitive framework. It represents an interface between linguistics and literature and develops a 6-tier theoretical model which analyses the different factors contributing to the creation of figurative words and expressions.

By examining features ranging from language structure to figurative thought, cultural history, reference, narrative and the personal experience of authors, it develops a global overview of the processes involved. Due to its particularly innovative characteristics in literature, the theme of death is explored in relation to universal concepts such as love and time. These aspects are discussed in the light of well-known authors in comparative literature such as D.H. Lawrence, Simone De Beauvoir, Hermann Hesse and Jorge Luis Borges. The origins can involve complex conceptual mappings in figures of speech such as metaphor and symbolism. They are often at the roots of an author's personal desires or represent the search for answers to human existence.

This approach offers a wide variety of new ideas and research possibilities for postgraduate and research students in modern languages, linguistics and literature. It would also be of interest to academic researchers in these disciplines as well as the general public who would like to delve deeper into the relevant fields.

Richard Trim is Professor Emeritus in Linguistics at the University of Toulon, France. His interest in the study of figurative language covers a wide variety of fields including historical linguistics, contrastive linguistics and translation with the analysis of corpora in both political and literary discourse. He has published widely in these different areas in the form of journal articles, the editing of conference proceedings, book reviews and monographs.

Routledge Focus on Literature

Introduction to Digital Humanities
Enhancing Scholarship with the Use of Technology
Kathryn C. Wymer

Geomythology
How Common Stories are Related to Earth Events
Timothy J. Burbery

Re-Reading the Eighteenth-Century Novel
Studies in Reception
Jakub Lipski

Trump and Autobiography
Corporate Culture, Political Rhetoric, and Interpretation
Nicholas K. Mohlmann

Biofictions
Literary and Visual Imagination in the Age of Biotechnology
Lejla Kucukalic

Neurocognitive Interpretations of Australian Literature
Criticism in the Age of Neuroawareness
Jean-François Vernay

Mapping the Origins of Figurative Language in Comparative Literature
Richard Trim

Metaphors of Mental Illness in Graphic Medicine
Sweetha Saji & Sathyaraj Venkatesan

For more information about this series, please visit: https://www.routledge.com/Routledge-Focus-on-Literature/book-series/RFLT

Mapping the Origins of Figurative Language in Comparative Literature

Richard Trim

NEW YORK AND LONDON

First published 2022
by Routledge
605 Third Avenue, New York, NY 10158

and by Routledge
2 Park Square, Milton Park, Abingdon, Oxon, OX14 4RN

Routledge is an imprint of the Taylor & Francis Group, an informa business

© 2022 Richard Trim

The right of Richard Trim to be identified as author of this work has been asserted by him in accordance with sections 77 and 78 of the Copyright, Designs and Patents Act 1988.

All rights reserved. No part of this book may be reprinted or reproduced or utilised in any form or by any electronic, mechanical, or other means, now known or hereafter invented, including photocopying and recording, or in any information storage or retrieval system, without permission in writing from the publishers.

Trademark notice: Product or corporate names may be trademarks or registered trademarks, and are used only for identification and explanation without intent to infringe.

Library of Congress Cataloging-in-Publication Data
A catalog record for this title has been requested

ISBN: 978-1-032-13035-4 (hbk)
ISBN: 978-1-032-14052-0 (pbk)
ISBN: 978-1-032-13037-8 (ebk)

DOI: 10.4324/9781032130378

Typeset in Times New Roman
by MPS Limited, Dehradun

Contents

Preface   xi
Acknowledgements   xiii

1 Towards a Global Model of Figurative Origins   1

    1.1 Conceptual Mapping 1
    1.2 Overview of Mappings in Pandemic Poetry 2
    1.3 Cultural Versus Universal Features 4
    1.4 Linguistic Structures 8
    1.5 Poetic Licence 9

2 Figurative Creativity in Language Structure   11

    2.1 The Power of Figurative Language 11
    2.2 Old and New Words 13
    2.3 Composite Structures 14
    2.4 Morpho-Syntax and Stylistic Effects 16
    2.5 Neologisms 17

3 Cross-Language Evidence for the Limits of Linguistic Creation   19

    3.1 Linguistic Relativity 19
    3.2 Translating Language Structures 20
    3.3 Language Distance 21
    3.4 Innovative Morphology 22
    3.5 Metaphor Versus Simile 24
    3.6 Dating Translation 25

3.7 Composite Order and Semantics 26
3.8 Symbolic Features 27

4 Underlying Figurative Thought   30

4.1 Cross-Language Imagery 30
4.2 Cognitive Theories 31
4.3 Individual Conceptualisation 33
4.4 Cognitive Linguistics 34
4.5 Metaphor and Symbol 35
4.6 Cognitive and Conflictual Paradigms 38

5 Tracing Cultural History   43

5.1 Diachronic Conceptual Networking 43
5.2 Diachronic Salience 45
5.3 Historical Origins of Figurative Words 46
5.4 The Love/Death Conceptual Metaphor 47
5.5 Understanding Figurative Language in Early Modern English 51

6 Theories of Reference in Conceptual Mapping   55

6.1 Extra-Linguistic Reference 55
6.2 Mental Spaces 56
6.3 Possible Worlds and Discourse Worlds 57
6.4 Reference in Conceptual Mappings 58
6.5 Philosophy and Reference 60
6.6 Hidden Reference Theory 61
6.7 Textual Reference 61

7 Textual Reference in the Form of Narrative   65

7.1 Variants of Love 65
7.2 Social Attitudes in D. H. Lawrence 66
7.3 Existentialism in Simone De Beauvoir 68
7.4 Personal Psychology in Hermann Hesse 70

8 Personal Biography in Figurative Language 75

8.1 Narrative and Personal Biography 75
8.2 "Distortion" of Personal Lives 76
8.3 Criticism of Biographical Theories 77
8.4 Autobiography and Autofiction 78
8.5 Individual Biographies 79
8.6 Symbolic Influence in D. H. Lawrence 79
8.7 The Philosophical Background to Simone De Beauvoir 82
8.8 Freudian Psychology in Hermann Hesse 84
8.9 Real and Non-Real Worlds 86

9 Conceptualisation of the Real World 89

9.1 Time Trajectories in Literal Meaning 89
9.2 Multicultural Conceptualisation of Time and Space 91
9.3 Time and Space in Literary Thought 92
9.4 Conceptualisation and Beliefs in Emily Dickinson 94

10 The Transformation of Reality 99

10.1 The Venezuelan Poet Eugenio Montejo 99
10.2 Transfigured Time 101
10.3 Time Symbolism and Language Structure 102
10.4 Switching Between Past and Future 104
10.5 New Spatial Forms 104
10.6 Notions of Real Worlds 105

11 Multiple Conceptual Mapping 107

11.1 The Symbolic Notion of "The South" in Jorge Luis Borges 107
11.2 The Background to Borges' Life 108
11.3 Narratological Conceptual Mappings 109
11.4 Language-Specific Symbolism in Borges 112
11.5 Fantasy and the Defiance of Death 113

12 The Overall Picture 115

References 121
Glossary of Linguistic Terms 129
Index 131

Preface

Due to a long-standing interest in the history of figurative language, the idea behind this book grew out of the search for its origins. The aim of the present study, however, is not to look for historical sources at a given point of time in the past but rather to investigate how figurative ideas develop in the mind of the person who creates and uses them. The same process can operate at any time in history. The world of figurative language is not only extremely powerful in literary discourse, it also demonstrates the outstanding creativity of the human mind. A great deal of ground has been covered in this direction within the framework of cognitive linguistics. On the basis of this discipline, we now know a lot more about processes operating in the underlying figurative structures of language and this framework has been adopted for the present study.

A major aim of the book, however, is to go beyond linguistic and textual information. The rationale behind the research is to trace figurative language back to the personal experience of the person producing it and, in this case, to the mind of a particular author. It thereby represents an interface between linguistics and literature. The thesis of the arguments put forward here is that, in a very large proportion of literary output, the figurative language used by protagonists in specific scenarios of a narrative reflects the personal experience of the author. Although this type of information is not always available in literary criticism, many links become apparent when biographical aspects come to light. These sources no doubt hold the key to the ultimate origins of a large proportion of figurative language.

The arguments are based on the proposal of a theoretical model comprising the major factors which influence a writer's choice of ideas and words. By adopting a comparative approach, it is also apparent that not only culture but also language structure play a role in the types of figurative language used. This becomes clear when the process of translation is taken into consideration. In other words, the language a writer uses may determine the options of figurative structures available and their corresponding creativity in a poem or novel.

Within this framework, the following comparative approach investigates a number of authors in world literature from different cultural and linguistic backgrounds. They include, among others, well-known names such as D.H. Lawrence, Hermann Hesse, Simone De Beauvoir, Emily Dickinson and Jorge Luis Borges. One major theme explored in this comparative approach is the notion of death and how ideas are mapped from or onto it. The theme was originally chosen for its innovative conceptual mappings in literature. They tend to be quite different from the everyday expressions described in studies within the cognitive field. At the time of writing, the world-wide Covid pandemic was in full force and daily figures of Covid-related deaths started appearing in the media. This reinforced the choice of the theme. For this reason, it was decided to begin the book by illustrating the general outlines of a theoretical model based on a selection of poetry associated with the epidemic. The theme of death is later linked to the universal notions of love and time. The former is often associated with impossible relationships due to factors such as society, individual psychology or philosophy. The latter may be used by authors to try and find the reasons for the very existence of an individual writer.

The book represents a brief insight into the different features involved in the roots of figurative language. It can be seen that multiple conceptual mapping, which takes place during the writing of a scenario, may be vast and goes deep into the creative mind of writers. It is hoped this global approach to figurative origins will help point the way to future avenues of similar research in both linguistics and literature.

Richard Trim
May 2021

Acknowledgements

I would like to thank Professors Ray Gibbs and Zoltán Kövecses for reading the first draft of the manuscript and for providing me with their invaluable comments and encouragement.

My thanks are also due to Commissioning Editor Jennifer Abbot and Editorial Assistant Mitchell Manners at Routledge for their organisational work involved in the publication of this book.

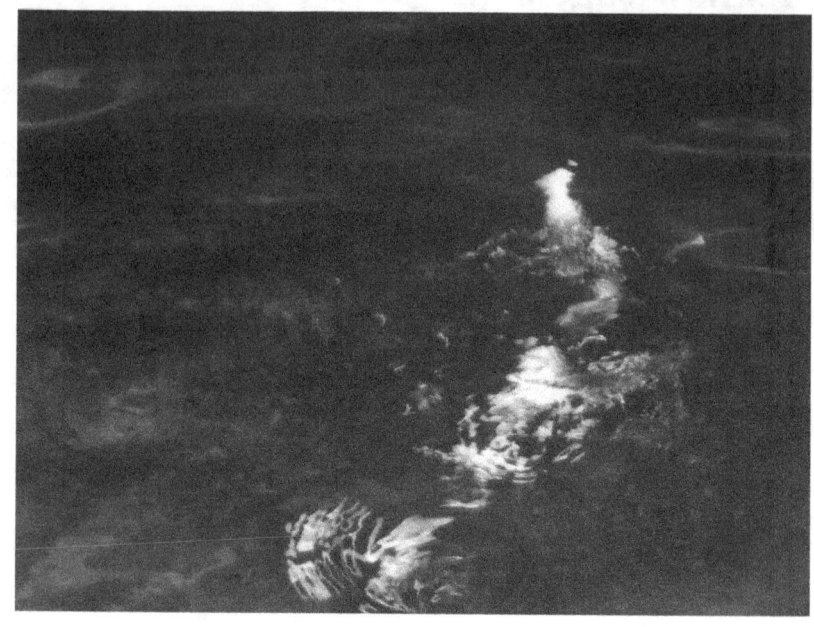

Figure 0.1 The Shattered Moon.
Photograph by Richard Trim.

1 Towards a Global Model of Figurative Origins

1.1 Conceptual Mapping

In order to delve into the different paths the human mind takes to create figurative language, the notion of conceptual mapping will be considered here in a larger context than the one in which an image is directly transferred from a source to target domain in the creation of a figurative expression. Within the framework of cognitive metaphor studies,[1] an example of this direct mapping would be a word such as 'ex-flame'. The meaning of a former love in this case implies the notion of heat, in the image of a flame, which is transferred to the target domain of love. According to cognitive linguists, there is an underlying conceptual metaphor which can be formulated in the equation: LOVE IS HEAT.[2]

At the same time, the human mind is able to access other types of transfer processes in the creation of figurative expressions. This may be either simultaneous or in succession according to the time it takes to select words in writing. Mental transfer in this wider sense includes the shift of one setting in the mind to another. A simple example would be the case of trying to fall asleep after a day's work. The brain continues to think about the day's problems at work and may cause insomnia. The substitution of the present setting to another, in which more relaxing thoughts come to mind, induce sleep more easily. This wider sense of transfer will also be referred to as a conceptual mapping. One setting, as well as an event within a specific setting, is mapped onto another world. The different types of conceptual mappings available in the mind help create the foundations of figurative language.

In literary discourse, the forms and structures that materialise depend on the experience, needs and desires of the writer. Origins are

DOI: 10.4324/9781032130378-1

2 Towards a Global Model

very often rooted in this initial personal experience. Although the inner thoughts of a writer cannot always be known, or are not necessarily autobiographical, a perusal of many standard literary works shows that there is very often an association with personal experience. This could even be linked to a personal interest in writing a genre such as science fiction.

Conceptual mapping from the author's experience is mapped further onto a narrative. This may be very short, as in the case of a poem consisting of a few lines. A poem often comprises a central theme depicted in the form of a symbol or metaphor which, in turn, acts as a focal point for the creation of related figurative expressions throughout the text. The expressions refer to specific persons or events in the narrative. Furthermore, the structure of figurative concepts is generally dependent on the cultural environment and historical period. They usually consist of an underlying conceptual mapping in figurative thought, as in the love and heat metaphor described above. Finally, ideas are put into linguistic forms which may often depend on the structures of the language used.

On this basis, a theoretical model of figurative origins will be proposed here. It consists of six major parameters which emerge from these conceptual mappings: 1) personal experience (or general biography of an author); 2) the creation of a narrative; 3) people, themes and events in discourse which represent the referential points of figurative mappings; 4) the environment of cultural history in which the author is writing; 5) figurative thought represented by underlying equations directly linked to expressions in a text and, finally, 6) the linguistic items themselves. All influences, starting with the first parameter of personal experience, help build figurative expressions in literary discourse. Any number, or all of the parameters subsequent to personal experience, form a part of figurative production.

1.2 Overview of Mappings in Pandemic Poetry

A preliminary illustration of this proposed model can be seen in a small selection of online poems which were recently published at the time of writing. These highlight individual influences on conceptual mapping and their creation in figurative language.[3] The poems, taken from the online publication of *Viral Verses*,[4] were written by poets from different backgrounds in Great Britain during the initial stages of the SARS-CoV-2 (severe acute respiratory syndrome), or Covid, pandemic. The spread of Covid greatly affected their lives, and poets wrote down their personal experiences during the 2020 period. Some poems described huge personal losses such as friends who succumbed to the epidemic. The poem written by Stephen Linstead, entitled *Curtains*,[5] describes such a loss. Thoughts are conveyed in figurative forms but directly reflect the reality and events that occurred in the poet's life.

Curtains (for Edward Tudor Crum)

Through the crack in the curtains
I dimly, without attention,
Discern that a van is reversing
And we should steer clear.
Flickering, my mournful tablet
Shows a leathery hand – old, strong,
Fingers full of music
Touching a tiny one
With love and delicacy
Met by a curious fist
Clutching for wisdom.
It's a hand I once grasped and found full
Of friendship, fun, foolishness
Skill and street wise laughter
And the will to keep a smile going
On our absurd mirthless journey.
We giggled our way through the white peak
On a cloud of herbs
In paroxysms at the silly sound
Of exotic words like paw-paw
On our urban English tongues.
We played and sang and danced
And clocked the devil's time sheet
With wistful wasteshifts that return unsquandered
In the memories that now repay me.
We took different roads but could hear each other
Just out of sight over the hill
A crested hill, with sun on both sides
And joyful other company
Until the long descent brought our footsteps together
And we hugged. We'd never hugged before.
We'd never hug again.
He's gone to the plague that pushes us apart
Leaving only echoed happiness

And my curtains shut as though
My soul can't bear the sunshine.

(Stephen Linstead)

The central theme of the poem is about the death of a friend, Edward Tudor Crum, to whom the poem is dedicated. The poet describes the memories of their friendship. Personal experience is a fundamental origin in the language of the poem and induces the reader to relive the scenario. In turn, it leads to a narrative which describes the different events that occurred. Activities included playing music, dancing and singing or "giggling our way through the white peak on a cloud of herbs". The narrative is full of references. It refers primarily to the two friends with pronouns such as "I", "we", etc. and the events in their lives.

The cultural setting is a modern one since the poem uses the image of a 'flickering mournful tablet'. The personification of this concept, which shows the symbol of friendship in the form of a "leathery hand", is obviously a modern technological image containing memories. The sad tablet relives pictures of a lost friend with a flickering light.

The figurative interpretation of this modern image may lead to a conceptual metaphor with a basic equation such as MEMORIES ARE A TABLET. The source domain of memories, in the form of photographs or videos on a screen, are mapped onto the target domain involving the personification of a device showing photographs. An extended conceptual metaphor, evoking the emotion of sadness, may be interpreted as SAD MEMORIES ARE A FLICKERING MOURNFUL TABLET. The equation thereby leads to the actual expression in the text.

1.3 Cultural versus Universal Features

Within the poem, there are also examples of more universal mapping trends in such equations. These tend to contrast with the cultural aspect. One major theme is the notion of life being a journey. The poem suggests life was an "absurd, mirthless journey" and the two friends took 'different roads'. However, they remained in contact since they could "hear each other".

These examples lead to a common conceptual metaphor in Western society, LIFE IS A JOURNEY, which has often been described within the framework of cognitive linguistics.[6] Many images of passing events in life are seen in the form of a journey, and this structure has been used in literature for a very long time. Indeed, the metaphor goes back as far as Antiquity:

> Spirits are assigned to less burdensome bodies on the journey of life
>
> (Boetius, *Consolatio Philosophiae*, 3, 19)

An oft-cited quote of this metaphor can be seen in Dante's work when the protagonist in the Divine Comedy is in the early stages of his descent into Hell:

> In the middle of life's road I found myself in a dark wood
>
> (Dante, *Divine Comedy, Purgatorio*, 1, 1–2).

Another form of more universal mapping is the visual perception of light and darkness. The former refers to positive qualities such as happiness and the latter to negative aspects like sadness. Hence, the symbol of curtains in the poem blocks out sunlight during a period of bereavement.

On this basis, the figurative language described in the poem originates in the form of 1) personal experience in losing a friend; 2) a short narrative being built up on past events associated with the friend; 3) reference points such as personal pronouns to denote the people involved in the figurative mappings; 4) cultural, as well as more universal, trends in the ideas expressed; 5) the use of these features in the underlying conceptual metaphors of figurative thought and 6) the creation of linguistic expressions in the text based on such conceptual metaphors.

Another example by the same poet, which illustrates this format of conceptual mappings, is the poem, *The Prospect Behind Us*[7]:

> The Prospect Behind Us
>
> Like a pantomime villain
> Or hoodied mugger
> Our future is behind us
> Creeping up unseen
> Beladen with chickens
> Coming home to roost
> Bulging briefcases of dog-eared

6   Towards a Global Model

> Accounts to be reckoned with
> Beneficient sacks of serendipity
> And whatever's coming to us.
> Whichever direction we look in
> The traumatic thaumaturge
> Is always behind us
> Whilst the pantomime audiences of history
> Scream hysterical indecipherable warnings
> As our befuddled faces peer.
> It has no reflection in life's rear-view mirror
> And never shows up on our mindless selfies
> Of self-consciousness.
> We don't back away from the future
> We just back into it
> And when it arrives
> We deny that the ships have come in
> Or pretend that the tawdry eagles have landed
> With feathers intact
> Or try to send it packing
> With ears full of exhausted fleas
> Whilst we gaze into the hollows
> Of the dark auditorium
> Struggling to perceive what hides in past light.
> And if through shifting scenes
> We nimbly avoid fate's sudden trapdoor
> We can't slink off into the wings
> Unanchored by its haunting shadow
> Or the gelled light that leaks
> Fuzzily focused from out of frame.
> We can't step forward beyond proscenium play
> Into knowledge.
> For all our props and make-up
> Idiots' tales and pyrotechnics
> We are puppets without strings
> And always, ever, becoming from behind.
>
> *(Stephen Linstead)*

A first reading of the poem reveals the fact that there are many examples of figurative language to describe the Covid pandemic. A central theme is the symbolic representation of the virus being a "pantomime villain" and the setting is within the environment of a theatre. The poet's personal experience of the virus is a feeling that the virus is invisible and creeps up on people like a "hoodied mugger". This invisibility, expressed in many ways throughout the poem, creates a narrative in which the victims of the virus are the actors on a stage. The helplessness of the victims can be seen in lines such as: "struggling to perceive what hides in past light", "we nimbly avoid fate's sudden trapdoor" or "we can't step forward beyond proscenium play into knowledge".

The referential points of figurative mappings are therefore the helpless actors themselves. A number of cultural aspects help form metaphors and symbols. As in the case of the previous poem, modern society and technology provides some good examples: "life's rear-view mirror" or "mindless selfies of self-consciousness". Conceptual metaphors may be extrapolated from these examples in an innovative way. The concept of time is reversed with the future in the past. Interpretations of a conceptual metaphor regarding the first example could be suggested as FUTURE IS A REAR-VIEW MIRROR, which is extended to the notion of life in the linguistic metaphor. In the same vein, a base conceptual metaphor of the second example could be SELF-CONSCIOUSNESS IS A SELFIE. This is semantically extended to the connotation of selfies being mindless, as expressed in the linguistic metaphor.

To summarise the six parameters with a few examples taken from the poem, the first one of personal experience involves the poet's feelings of the virus being invisible. The second develops a narrative in which these feelings are mapped onto a theatrical scene. The third parameter of referential points involves the mapping of the theatrical scene onto the actors themselves. This is highlighted with the use of personal pronouns such as "we" and "us". The fourth influence of culture is found in the mapping of modern technology onto target-domain images. Fifth, the latter are mapped onto equations in the form of suggested conceptual metaphors such as SELF-CONSCIOUSNESS IS A SELFIE. Sixth, the equations are mapped onto relevant linguistic metaphors in the text like "mindless selfies".

This scenario represents the basic format of the model in exploring origins. Other mental processes can be included within the six parameters. In this respect, two points should be made and can be illustrated with the poem, *The Prospect Behind Us*. The first is the role of target-language linguistic structures used to depict conceptual metaphors. This can be fairly straightforward, if the relevant linguistic knowledge is available, but may involve more complex issues such as the limits of creative linguistic evolution in a given language.

8 *Towards a Global Model*

The second is the part played by space and time orientation. Further analysis on these topics will be taken up in the following chapters. However, two brief examples may be given here.

1.4 Linguistic Structures

A language-specific expression in the poem would be "traumatic thaumaturge". It is obviously based on two words having similar phonetic structures. Similar sounds can reinforce stylistic effects, whether the expression is figurative or not. An extended example may be taken from another poem in *Viral Verses* with regard to acronyms. It is entitled *NHS* by Paul Thwaites.[8] The first verse will be cited here together with the first lines of the subsequent verses:

NHS

Now Heaven Sent our gentle warriors come,
No clarion calls to battle, no hollow drum,
Sounding its futile roll,
That spurs them through this vale of tears,
Releasing precious breath from captive air,
Where feathered death wings
Waiting on each soul
And does not spare,
These who have fallen on his spears.

No Heart Succumbs in fear...
New Heroes Serve, a new wind blows...
New Hope Survives, when marshalled by the brave ...
Nations Hear Songs before unheard...

(Paul Thwaites)

The acronym NHS, referring to the National Health Service in Great Britain, serves to denote the medical staff fighting the Covid epidemic within the context of a battlefield. The figurative expressions, ranging from 'warriors', 'clarion calls' and 'hollow drums' to 'vale of tears' and 'spears', are all related to the central symbol of the NHS. In this way, 'now heaven sent', 'no heart succumbs', etc. at the beginning of each verse, can reinforce the role of the NHS symbol. The conceptual mapping model reveals the experience and feelings of the poet towards the virus and medical staff. A narrative of a battle is developed, with the referents being the medical staff for the war terminology used. The NHS is a British cultural symbol. Conceptual metaphors appear such as NURSES ARE WARRIORS and are associated with the relevant linguistic items cited above.

The acronym in this form is only possible in English and, although the poem can, of course, be translated into another language, the stylistic force of this central feature would be lost. Consequently, a large number of important figurative expressions are specific to the words and linguistic structures of the language used.

1.5 *Poetic Licence*

The aspect of space and time orientation, which is very often central to figurative thought, can play a major role in mappings. Apart from historical or culture-specific variations in orientation, this study will concentrate on another dimension which updates knowledge about conventional cognitive models: the role of poetic licence in literary discourse. In the early days of cognitive linguistics, the focus on expressions in everyday language assumed that idealised cognitive models would naturally follow certain patterns. These would involve, for example, the future being in front, the past being behind and so on. In a very large proportion of logical, everyday expressions, this is undoubtedly the case: "I have a huge task in front of me"; "I'm glad I've put that behind me" and so on. However, this study will explore how conventional cognitive processes can also evolve into any number of conceptual mapping patterns within a literary context. A basic example in the poem, *The Prospect Behind Us,* and as the title suggests, is that the future is behind us.

On the basis of this six-tier model of conceptual mapping in the creation of figurative language, a deeper analysis of these parameters will be applied to the field of world literature. A useful starting point is the imaginative and creative writing of the author D. H. Lawrence.

Notes

1 See the seminal work on this theory in Lakoff & Johnson (1980). The model will be adopted for the analysis of corpora in this study. Capital letters are used in this approach to denote figurative mappings between source and target domains. It will be seen that a major distinction is made between the linguistic expression and the underlying figurative equation in conceptual mapping.

2 Kövecses (1988: 56–83).
3 I am indebted to Stephen Linstead for his permission to include analyses of poems from *Viral Verses. Art in Exceptional Times* [https://www.viralverses.com/].
4 Linstead (2020).
5 Ibid.: p. 18.
6 Op. cit. Lakoff & Johnson (1980).
7 Op. cit. Linstead (2020: 103).
8 Ibid.: 211.

2 Figurative Creativity in Language Structure

2.1 The Power of Figurative Language

The model of conceptual mapping discussed in the previous chapter outlines a progression of steps in cognition which arise from an author's personal experience to the figurative structures used in language. In order to look directly at common figures of speech in the literature, the model will now be turned upside down. In other words, the following discussions will first focus on language itself and then trace back the cognitive paths which have led to the linguistic expressions.

Figurative language is undoubtedly a powerful way of enhancing the narrative in literary discourse. As has been suggested, it often reveals information about the writer's inner thoughts and intentions. At the level of language, the words and expressions in literary works are the first contact the reader has of the writer's mind and potentially open the way to their ultimate origins. The writer develops a personal style which is reflected in the choice of linguistic structures available in the language used. As a result, the way these structures are applied in literature tends to have an impact on the reader's feelings about descriptions in the narrative. The writer can use ingenious ways of creating images that influence the imagination, thereby producing a powerful stylistic tool. Images are mapped onto concepts which show how the writer reflects on innovative ways of expressing thoughts. In turn, this innovation may be related to underlying and more hidden reasons for the events in a given scenario. They are thus the starting point to exploring clues leading to the origins of language structures and figurative meaning.

Powerful stylistic tools can be seen in the following passage. It is taken from the novel, *Women in Love,* by D. H. Lawrence, and the

DOI: 10.4324/9781032130378-2

description linked to the theme of love, reveals intense emotions in the scenes:

> He stood staring at the water. Then he stooped and picked up a stone, which he threw sharply at the pond. Ursula was aware of the bright moon leaping and swaying, all distorted, in her eyes. It seemed to shoot out arms of fire like a cuttle-fish, like a luminous polyp, palpitating strongly before her. And his shadow on the border of the pond, was watching for a few moments, then he stooped and groped on the ground. Then again there was a burst of sound, and a burst of brilliant light, the moon had exploded on the water, and was flying asunder in flakes of white and dangerous fire. Rapidly, like white birds, the fires all broken rose across the pond, fleeing in clamorous confusion, battling with the flock of dark waves that were forcing their way in. The furthest waves of light, fleeing out, seemed to be clamouring against the shore for escape, the waves of darkness came in heavily, running under towards the centre. But at the centre, the heart of all, was still a vivid, incandescent quivering of a white moon not quite destroyed, a white body of fire writhing and striving and not even now broken open, not yet violated.
>
> *Women in Love*, D.H. Lawrence[1]

The scene continues for several pages in the novel. The language and imagery of the text contain stark expressions such as "a burst of brilliant light", "flying asunder" and "clamorous confusion". Individual concepts are represented by various figures of speech. The passage reveals that the major symbol is the moon which is personified by its leaping and swaying. It is linked to other figurative concepts such as metaphoric fire or similes, as in cuttle-fish, polyps and so on. Apart from the mere representation of these figures of speech, the act of throwing a stone into the pond and disrupting the moon's reflection on the water is an attempt to eliminate the presence of the symbol. It is an important feature in the narrative and indicates what thoughts are going through the protagonist's mind. It can be seen that, as the rippling waves on the water start to subside, the symbol has not been entirely destroyed. Eliminating the symbolic image is difficult and appears to upset the person who threw the stone into the pond. This particular event and its scenario, which represent another clue in the search for origins beyond the level of language, will be discussed in more detail below.

Figurative language contains a vast number of stylistic forms such as the symbolism, personification or metaphors used in the passage above, or various linguistic categories as in metonymy, phraseology and so on. They are represented in different components of language structures as in phonetics, semantics, morpho-syntax, etc., either individually or in combination. All contribute to the creation of figurative models.

2.2 Old and New Words

This study will focus, in particular, on metaphor and symbol. Differences between the two will be debated in the next chapter, but one important aspect about figurative use should be mentioned at the outset: both metaphor and symbol, as well as other types of figures of speech such as phraseology, are usually applied according to three possible criteria. One is that a word or expression already exists in the language so that figurative use tends to be conventional according to items in the standard language. Basic dictionary entries at any one point in time may be modified to a certain extent. Using an extension of the 'ex-flame' example cited in the previous chapter, "his old flame was finally extinguished" would mean his former love finally came to an end. In this example, the word 'flame' for a loved one is a relatively standard expression.

The second point is that an item may be a very individualised creation which can involve both changes in linguistic structure, as well as imagery. This is a typical feature in literary discourse. However, such changes tend to be confined to the outer structural and conceptual limits of the language concerned, otherwise the item would not make sense, even when the context is taken into account.

A third feature is a cross-cultural perspective in which the use of structure or imagery may not necessarily make sense, unless the reader is well acquainted with the foreign language and culture. All these features will be taken up in the theories discussed below.

Conventional figures of speech do not normally present a problem with regard to interpretation and, in some cases, they may have a more universal, or at least a predominantly cross-cultural, slant to them. As was suggested in the previous chapter, this often occurs when physiological factors are involved. Individualised creations tend to vary much more in their interpretation. They may be very easy to understand, and perhaps used in everyday conversation, or they could stand out due to their idiosyncratic nature. The following discussion will begin by looking at the field of morpho-syntax in individualised and more personal expressions. In particular, compound (or composite) grammatical structures will be examined in the symbolic themes used by D.H. Lawrence.[2] The focus on morpho-syntax throughout this book will include primarily different types of morphological derivation as well as figurative use of verbal structures. In this way, morphological derivation can add further clues as to origins. The next passage, with composites in bold type, demonstrates the frequent use of compounding in Lawrence's novel, *The Rainbow*:

> They went towards the stackyard. There he saw, with something like terror, the great new stacks of corn glistening and gleaming transfigured, silvery and present under the **night-blue** sky, throwing dark substantial shadows, but themselves majestic and dimly present. She, like glimmering gossamer, seemed to burn among them, as they rose like cold fires to the **silvery-bluish** air. All was intangible, a burning of cold, glimmering, **whitish-steely** fires. He was afraid of the **moon-conflagration** of the cornstacks rising above him. His heart grew smaller, it began to fuse like a bead. He knew he would die.
>
> *The Rainbow*, D.H. Lawrence[3]

The narrative of this novel involves three generations of the Brangwen family in the East Midlands of England at the beginning of the twentieth century. It describes how different love relationships of the Brangwens change throughout the period of increasing industrialisation in Britain at the time. The major part of the plot deals with a daughter in the family, again with the name of Ursula, who struggles to find fulfilment in love and finally enters a passionate but doomed love affair with Anton Skrebensky, a British soldier of Polish descent. This particular passage evokes a very powerful scene when the two lovers dance at a village festival and afterwards go for a walk among the haystacks in the moonlight. Lawrence increases the austere atmosphere of the difficult romantic encounter by using compound metaphors reflecting the deep emotions portrayed by the symbol of the moon.

2.3 Composite Structures

The compound structures tend to become more innovative and idiosyncratic with each line in the paragraph. The first two, 'night-blue' and 'silvery-bluish', are relatively standard and conventional in their use of colours. 'Whitish-steely', however, is more innovative, blending the colour of the moonlight with the harsh image of steel. Even more innovative is the composite noun 'moon-conflagration', as if there is a fire on the moon which lights up the surrounding haystacks. The combination of the opposing concepts of coldness and fire equally add to the austere scene.

The use of compound metaphors stylistically reinforces the foreboding nature of the encounter. Lawrence is able to manipulate English morphology in this typical style which would often be considered non-standard in English grammar. Such is the example of another description from the novel relating to the shyness of a girl in the story. The feature is combined with the symbolic nature of violets in *The Rainbow*:

> Emily? Little, shy-violet sort of girl with nice eyebrows

The inversion of 'shy' and 'violet' in a compound which usually requires 'shy' as the second morpheme in attribute adjectives, as in 'work-shy', is more idiosyncratic and stands out more as a figure of speech. However, the latter order would create a different meaning such as 'averse to violets', as in 'averse to work'. The combination of 'shy' with the symbolic feature of violets, as in the semantic field of love relationships, reinforces the overall meaning of the compound. From a syntactic point of view, Lawrence changes around word order in composite adjectives which may normally be standard in simple noun phrases.

This is the case of another form of inversion in the case of the metaphoric innovation "flame-lurid", as in "flame-lurid his face". This expression, although understandable, would probably not be used naturally in everyday conversation, even during Lawrence's day. It has been suggested that the inversion of the noun and adjective in the compound, as compared to the normal noun phrase, "a lurid flame", is a figurative innovation used by Lawrence to attract the reader's attention to a concept often symbolised by natural forces:[4]

> **Flame-lurid** his face as he turned among the throng of flame-lit and dark faces upon the platform. In the light of the furnace she caught sight of his drifting countenance, like a piece of floating fire. And the nostalgia, the doom of homecoming went through her veins like a drug. His eternal face, **flame-lit** now! The pulse and darkness of red fire from the **furnace towers** in the sky, lighting the desultory, industrial crowd on the wayside station, lit him and went out.
>
> Frank and Annie, D.H. Lawrence[5]

There is an extension of this composite in the term "flame-lit". The "furnace towers", another clue to figurative origins and a key feature in the writer's mind, will be discussed in more detail below. It represents an

16 *Figurative Creativity*

important aspect of environmental settings in Lawrence's writing. The concept of fire, a natural force like the moon-conflagration example mentioned above, is linked to the appearance of the face on the station platform in the scene from *Frank and Annie*. Other examples of natural forces are apparent in the stylistic inversion of compounds such as: "cyclamen leaves, toad-filmy, earth-iridescent",[6] terms taken from Lawrence's poem *Sicilian Cyclamens*.[7]

Some literary critics suggest that inversion attracts the reader's attention to a concept which often symbolises natural forces. Apart from this particular explanation, inversion is a frequent stylistic tool used by Lawrence, and it might indeed be to focus on one image in the compound, more than the other. In this case, it would be "flame", as it comes first. From a deeper literary point of view, which requires explanations regarding Lawrence's personal background, as discussed in more detail in chapter 7, some critics suggest that the use of compounds in general stems from his anti-imperialist views that can be found in his poetry. This is also linked to Lawrence's relationship with nature which often involves inversion as well.

Consequently, Lawrence appears to criticize the reasoning of an imperialist system imposed on nature. This can be in the form of historical monuments built after military conquests, and so on. The expression "cyclamen leaves [...] earth-iridescent" therefore implies that "light is filtered by a material which is not entirely transparent". The cyclamen leaves retain their integrity and only reflect the light of nature around them. The term "iridescent" metaphorically signifies a resistance to outside interference with nature in the form of imperialist buildings and so on, thereby reinforcing his anti-imperialist feelings.

2.4 Morpho-Syntax and Stylistic Effects

The result is that double or multiple images in such metaphors reinforce the atmosphere of the different scenes in the narrative. Natural forces are one source in Lawrence's writing. Another suggested source in compound adjectives appears to be historical or religious contexts.[8] A case in point is the word 'quick'. The standard meaning of speed or completing a task in a short amount of time becomes unclear in Lawrence's idiosyncratic expressions: 'unquick', 'father-quick', 'mother-quick', and so on. These occur in many of his novels. It appears that this literary meaning of 'quick' is based on the Biblical notion whereby the living are associated with the dead, as in 'the quick and the dead' (Peter 4:35). Lawrence tended to change the root word into different semantic variations such as the neologism

Figurative Creativity 17

"unquick", i.e. "dead". The semantic complexity of this case is illustrated further by etymological considerations. Old English *cwic* (living) was metaphorised into the sense of speed and its related present-day variations. Furthermore, the original 'living' sense has been retained in certain fixed expressions such as 'cut to the quick' with its related sense of 'hurting someone emotionally'. This finding in compound figurative expressions shows that cultural history, combined with the aspect of historical linguistics in lexical analysis, are also vital in the search for figurative origins.

2.5 Neologisms

The morphological structures of English appear to be particularly open to composite innovation which goes a long way beyond standard norms in the language. Poetic licence is evidence for this, as can be seen in the following poem by E.E. Cummings:

> Which when both
> march outward into the freezing fire of Thickness) points
> uPDownishly
> find everywheres noise-coloured
> curvecorners gush silently perpetuating solids (More fluid than gas
> *the surely,* E.E. Cummings[9]

In this poem, it can be seen that composites are created freely with examples such as "noise-coloured curvecorners". In addition, morphological derivation has nearly no limits as in "uPDownishly", which also includes non-standard orthography in capital letters. Furthermore, it can be seen that Cummings was particularly interested in colours and shapes. The fact that the poet was an artist suggests that the figurative thoughts in his mind involve the juxtaposing of concepts in language, in the same way as colours and shapes in paintings. This style is typical of his poems which is not always easy to interpret without context. The linguistic style can become quite abstract and, as in the case of art, becomes open to interpretation.

Neologisms of this kind tend to form an important part of poetry, and there appear to be different types. One proposed categorisation of neologisms, similar to the three aspects discussed above regarding conventional and non-conventional use, includes the following: first, those which have no dictionary entries; second, recent innovations; third, those which are semantically unstable and, fourth, expressions which appear to be new to the reader.[10] In poetic licence, all these may contribute to non-standard forms but, in this particular case of neologisms, many would probably be new to the reader. Consequently, the issue of comprehension would no doubt depend on context. This may be related to the length of the poem which is long enough to supply enough background information. However, certain composites may be intrinsically easier to understand than others, depending on the types of links to existing linguistic and conceptual phenomena.

To summarise, a preliminary finding in the foregoing discussion is that the way in which figurative language enhances feelings and emotions in a narrative depends on different types of use in language structure and imagery. These are available to the writer within the limits of linguistic and conceptual innovation. The approach adopted here is that the preliminary step of linguistic analysis represents the starting point in exploring where figurative language comes from. In the case of English, there seems to be a fairly large potential for innovation in which images can be placed side-by-side in the form of compounding in lexical items. This is an important case for stylistic force with regard to other figures of speech such as similes. For example, it has been suggested that metaphors are more forceful and more profound than similes.[11] The reason given is that the conceptual links between source and target domains of the metaphoric mapping can be re-used and incorporated into various innovative extensions within the same lexeme. This is not necessarily the case with similes which tend to simply state comparisons.

In the next chapter, the level of language will be explored further with regard to cross-language structures. These can reveal considerable differences in morpho-syntactic and semantic features. In other words, the argument proposed here is that the language used will create different types of figurative patterns.

Notes

1 Lawrence (1920, chapter 19).
2 For more information regarding the influence of language structure on the creation of metaphor and symbol, see Trim (2018a, 2018b, 2019).
3 Lawrence (1915, chapter 11).
4 Niven (1978: 2).
5 Lawrence (1922).
6 Bouttier (2013: para. 33).
7 Lawrence (1923).
8 Brault-Dreux (2013: para. 31).
9 Cummings (1972).
10 Mejri and Sablayrolles (2011: para. 6); Cabré (1992, 2004).
11 Zharikov and Gentner (2002: 976).

3 Cross-Language Evidence for the Limits of Linguistic Creation

3.1 Linguistic Relativity

If the entire range of potential language structures is examined, it is essential to look outside one particular language. Even closely related languages reveal major differences. An examination of the language – structure layer in the six-tier model proposed reveals some of this potential in a cross-cultural approach. In addition, this aspect is closely linked to the underlying layer of figurative thought and its cultural implications. The close interaction raises a number of issues.

The extent to which language structure may condition human thought has been the subject of controversy for a long time. It includes the theory of linguistic relativity,[1] which claims that language has a considerable impact on thought. Recent views suggest that two variants are possible. The first is a strong one, claiming that language *determines* our way of thinking. The second is a weaker version which opts for the idea that it *influences* thought. Today, many scholars think the latter is more realistic since the former would prevent us from learning foreign languages. However, this area of research still requires a substantial amount of investigation.[2]

The theory proposed here is that language structures can actually influence what kind of figurative forms a writer uses and that they have an impact on stylistic force. In a nutshell, the argument is that the language used, due to its particular linguistic (as well as conceptual) structures, has an influence on figures of speech. All types, together with their linguistic components, may be included in such a claim.

The example of composites in morpho-syntax will be analysed here at a deeper, cross-language level. One useful tool in this respect is the process of translation. The potential for translating an item is

DOI: 10.4324/9781032130378-3

dependent on the same types of poetic licence, which would be feasible in a target language. This aspect has been investigated by a number of different linguists in translation studies and whose ideas will be included in the debate below. The aim of this comparison, however, is not to discuss translation techniques *per se* but to demonstrate how their constraints reveal cross-language differences in morpho-syntactic innovation.

3.2 Translating Language Structures

With this in mind, would it be possible to translate all the neologisms in Cummings' poem, discussed in the previous section, into another language while keeping the same style? The task appears to be extremely difficult. The following discussion will investigate their translation into French.

The first difficulty is that, as far as composites are concerned, French is a Latinate-based language, whereas the morpho-syntax of English still retains its basic Germanic forms. This means that French is an analytical language in which relationships between phrasal units are normally conveyed by the means of connectors such as prepositions and particles. Although this occurs in English, particularly since its breakdown from the more agglutinative period of Old English due to French influence in the Middle Ages, it still retains a considerable capacity to combine morphemes into multiple composites. One extreme example in English is the following title:

> How conservatives Turned Liberalism into a Tax-Raising, Latte-drinking, Sushi-eating, Volvo-driving, New-York Times-Reading, Body-Piercing, Hollywood-Loving, Left-Wing Freak Show.[3]

Apart from attempting to convey cultural aspects, the same linguistic structures would be impossible in French. In most cases, the composites would have to be translated by relative clauses such as "those who love Hollywood" (*ceux qui aiment Hollywood*) rather than "Hollywood-loving". This would also apply to prepositional phrases in fixed expressions such as "of left" (*de gauche*) for "left-wing". The stylistic effect in English is the repetition of gerund forms in the composites which are thereby lost in French. Consequently, the concepts could be literally translated in some form or other, but the main aim of the style disappears.

With regards to Cummings' poem, a similar problem arises in compounds, such as "noise-coloured", which would have to be rendered as "the colour of noise" (*couleur de bruit*). Once again, the main aim of Cummings' style in his use of composites would be completely lost. This aspect raises the question of structural distance between languages and how it affects style. Before looking at ways of translating Cummings' poetry and the feasibility of producing the same figurative language, a brief comment on his ideas regarding language structure is needed.

Cummings, as an artist and poet, produced innovations in English poetry which, as pointed out above, seem similar to creations in his paintings. He appears to have introduced linguistic innovations along the same lines as the Russian poet, Mayakovsy,[4] who was equally both an artist and poet. They appeared to blur the line between the two forms of their art forms and "foreshadowed the digital revolution of today in their multimedia experiments in poetry".[5] Politically, they worked in totally different environments. Cummings criticised the Soviet system of the time for its suppression of individual and artistic freedom while Mayakovsky complained that the West's capitalist system retarded the development of art. He claimed that Russia had the advantage after the Revolution of casting off the old system to give way to new ideas and forms.[6]

According to such comparative studies on the two poets, the aspect of innovation in English and Russian appears to follow both compounding and the "loosening of syntactic ties". Since Russian "demands more grammatical subordination than English", the creation of lexemes independent of syntax is more noticeable in this particular language.[7] For example, Mayakovsy uses an isolated nominative case, (as in "night"), to set the image conveyed by the noun separate from the rest of the text: "Night. You put on the fanciest dress".[8]

3.3 Language Distance

The relationship between these two procedures and the degree of agglutination in a language probably requires further research. For example, the range of Russian declensions used in individual lexemes covering a large choice of innovations would be useful to support this argument. However, if the separation of morphemes is also a common process in artistic innovation independently of language choice, the strict rules of agglutination may therefore become less important in this form of literary discourse. The contrastive difference between agglutinative and less agglutinative (analytic) languages will be taken up here with regard to the problem of compounding in figurative creation and its limits regarding style and interpretation.

22 Cross-Language Evidence

Due to other lexical semantic considerations, it will be suggested that the potential for compounding on the grounds of analytic linguistic forms is not as straightforward as it may appear at first sight. Apart from French, comparisons will be made with the agglutinative languages of German and Russian, which would seem to be closer to the compounding potential found in English, in contrast to the more analytic Latinate languages. The argument here is that, even though English is normally categorised as an analytic language, the data here on metaphorical neologisms reveal that French is more analytic than English as far as compounding is concerned. The test is therefore to see if a Latinate language is capable of innovating the same composite forms.

3.4 Innovative Morphology

Various attempts have been made to translate Cummings' poetry into French. One attempt is by using more technical morphemes of Latin and Greek origin.[9] The following list contains a selection of Cummings' innovative compound adjectives. The interpretation of creations of this kind may depend on the reader's ability to link certain morphemes used in more technical contexts within the conceptual limits of the target language. The English versions use basic vocabulary, whereas the French composites use morphemes such as *acous-*, *gyné-* and *andro-*. These arguably represent a different style to Cummings' version:

noise-coloured	*acousmachrome*
sleep-shaped	*hypnomorphe*
women-coloured	*gynéchrome*
man-shaped	*andromorphe*
small-headed	*microcéphale*

It implies that a good knowledge of Latin and Greek roots is required for comprehension. The result is that the same levels of interpretation and style may be different between the languages and limit this kind of translation technique. It would thereby suggest that identical forms are not always possible. In the case of poetry, an additional problem arises in relation to poetic rhythm. An analysis of this feature shows that the attempt to translate the rhythm of compounds requires more searching for possible innovative terms. The following line demonstrates the translation of rhythm in neologisms by using similar morphemes (in bold type):

But straight glad feet **fearruining** and **glorygirded** faces

*Mais des pieds directs joyeux des visages **peurruinants** et **glorioréolés***

The levels of style and interpretation of the words appear to be maintained in this case, but the example shows that, on the one hand, the process is dependent on the degree of cognate relationship between the two languages. The rhythm of the compounds "fearruining"/ "*peurruinant*" (in the literal sense that feet are not afraid), is maintained by the consonant /r/ and the same cognate root word "ruin" supports it. This is almost pure chance since the latter is due to English "ruin" being loaned from Old French *ruine*. On the other hand, it is possible that identical root words may not be due to cognate etymology at all but to phonological proximity. This increases the arbitrary availability of compounding for the sake of rhythm. In the case of "fear"/"*peur*", they may originally come from the same Indo-European source, but the immediate ancestors were Germanic for English (Old English "*fǣr*") and Latin for French (*pavor*). The structural distance between language no doubt influences stylistic figures of speech. Cognate structures, and other cross-linguistic aspects that have similar phonological and morpho-syntactic features, are an important point in language-specific morphemic derivation. This is therefore the case in the creation of neologisms which may correspond in rhythm. However, it appears that, despite the similarities in the examples mentioned above, structural proximity is often arbitrary.

Similar problems of rhythm occur in individual cases. The term *glorioréolé* in French represents a very subtle invention for a neologism that translates 'glorygirded'. A morphemic and semantic breakdown of the term reveals the following facts. Two basic morphemes are blended: *glorie* (glory) and *auréolé* (crowned by a halo). The image is therefore one of having a halo whose Latin origin *aureola* signifies a halo of gold. The morpheme *–ola* originally comes from Greek *hálōs* (disk), as in English "halo". However, the term *gloriole* also exists, likewise linked to *glorie* and derived from a diminutive form in Latin *gloriola,* introduced as a pejorative term in the 18th century.[10] For this reason, the term *gloriolé* would not have been suitable, and it may be assumed that, perhaps for other reasons as well, an additional affix *–oré-* has been inserted to avoid the negative connotation. The result of this analysis is that, although there may be ways of creating similar metaphors between English and French in poetry of this kind, the different levels of interpretation, style and rhythm are complex and suggest that a metaphor in one language may have to be substituted for another form of figure of speech in another.

3.5 Metaphor Versus Simile

One argument which supports purely structural differences between agglutinative and analytic languages is the metaphor/simile distinction. It does appear that Latinate structures often require similes in conveying the same composite metaphoric image used in English. This can be seen in many fixed expressions such as "stonecold", "honeysweet" or "razor-sharp" which need to be expressed by structures in French such as *froid comme le marbre* (literally: cold like marble), *doux comme le miel* (sweet like honey), *tranchant comme un rasoir* (cutting like a razor), etc.[11] French does not have equivalent compound adjectives in its standard lexical stock with regard to such terms.

Furthermore, English compound adjectives possess a wide variety of syntactic combinations such as the basic adjective + adjective structure, as well as noun + adjective, noun + gerund and so on. In particular literary styles, structures and specific images are repeated for effect. In the case of the passage in *The Rainbow* in the previous chapter, colour and light are used in repeated syntactic constructions: "whitish-steely", "silvery-bluish", "silver-gleaming", etc. Stylistic force is thereby lost in another language if it does not have access to this syntactic repetition. One French translation of the passage comes up with the following structures in the relevant metaphors[12]:

a. *le ciel bleu de nuit* = the blue sky of night (night-blue sky)
b. *l'air bleu d'argent* = the blue air of silver (silvery-bluish air)
c. *des feux brûlaient tout en luisant comme du métal blanc et froid* = fires burning while glimmering like white and cold metal (whitish-steely fires)

The examples (a) and (b) require prepositional phrases in translation with postpositioning of one of the images, 'night' and 'silver' in these two cases, after the subject. The third example (c) requires paraphrasing with the aid of a synonym which is quite different from the original compound adjective. The contrast between the concepts of coldness and fire are reinforced in the combination of the compound adjective and noun, 'whitish-steely fires', and arguably does not have the same effect in the French translation due to repetition of this structure in the narrative. The double images are intended to merge together to give an overall austere impression of the concept and this effect is therefore lost.

Consequently, the contrastive linguistic approach to this argument shows that Latinate languages often require different single-concept structures such as similes and prepositional phrases to convey the same meaning of an original metaphor. Other languages like Italian and Spanish would no doubt reveal the same contrast with English. Double images in a metaphor are dispersed morpho-syntactically and thereby appear to reduce the power of merged images. This is particularly the case in the French translations cited above, which do not attempt, or cannot, create neological structures in the same way as the Latin/Greek innovations.

3.6 Dating Translation

If factors other than purely linguistic structure are considered, such as semantics and polysemy, cross-language variation tends to increase. Language distance is confronted with patterns in composites which have different parameters within syntactic ordering. At this point, one aspect of translated forms, apart from experimenting with neologisms in the target language, plays a part in the discussion on distance. This concerns either the dating of official literary translations or those produced by native-speaker assessment of target-language items. The use of syntactic structures in the translation of modals into French from Jane Austen's *Pride and Prejudice,* for example, tend to vary according to the date of the translation.[13] Such factors can depend on semantic and conceptual change through time, language use in specific contexts and diachronic syntactic change. The choice of language-specific innovation can also depend on individual native speakers who may assess possible translations in different ways.

The following examples of translation into different languages of Lawrence's compounding point out the variations. A comparison will be made with the other (synthetically classified) languages of German and Russian. There appear to be a number of official French translations of *The Rainbow* but fewer in German, and none appear to be available in Russian. In the latter case, native-speaker assessment is required to make the comparison. Official German examples date from 1964,[14] which may account for its more conservative structures. In other words, figurative neologisms in the target language tend to be avoided generally in the translation, and standard German morphology is maintained.

A case in point is Lawrence's "whitish-steely" described above. Technically, a German translation could imitate the English structure with *weisslich-stählern*. Indeed, a native-speaker assessment is as follows but without the hyphen in the compound:

> *Alles war unbegreiflich, ein Brennen kalter, glimmernder, **weisslich stählerner Feuer.*** [15]

> (All was intangible, a burning of cold, glimmering, **whitish-steely** fires.)

However, the composite has been modified to a certain extent in the following translation from 1964, and the two adjectives have been modified by "steely white" (*stählern weissen*):

> *Nichts war greifbar, alles war wie ein Brand aus kalten, glimmernden, **stählern weissen** Feuern.*

This diverges more in an assessment of Russian: сверкающий металлическим блеском (shining with metallic light).[16] With regard to the compound noun, "moon-conflagration", it appears to follow identical syntactic and conceptual patterns in a translated German equivalent: *Mondbrand* (moon-fire); but it seems to be conceptually different in Russian: озаренный лунным светом (dawned by moonlight).

Similar differences in translation appear with other compounds in Lawrence's novel, *The Rainbow*. Two expressions, which reveal different contextual situations, are "shy-violet" mentioned above and the innovatory metaphor, "salt-burning body".

3.7 Composite Order and Semantics

Despite the agglutinative nature of German morphology, the similar use of a compound adjective leads to a number of complications. The same syntactic order as in English would not only be non-standard but may also create problems of comprehension in German as in one hypothetical structure, (an asterisk indicating a non-standard form):

> Shy-violet sort of girl = *ein schüchtern-Veilchen-artiges Mädchen*

In addition, the semantic component complicates the use of the same compound in translation. In standard English and German, compounds based on noun+adjective are common features. The term "workshy", for example, corresponds to the German *arbeitsscheu*. However, this type of collocation does not always correspond.

Such combinations do not always exist between the standard lexis of the two languages, even if new creations calqued on the other language are comprehensible. The term *wasserscheu* (afraid of water) would sound strange in English *"watershy". A phrase such as "afraid of (going into) water" is more likely to be used if, for example, swimming activities are involved. In another register, such as in the case of medical or scientific language in general, a term like "hydrophobic" might be used. As in English described above, the final position of the morpheme in the compound, the cognate "shy/ *scheu*" is used in a large number of cases but with the sense of "fear" or "aversion" to something. As a result, the use of standard syntax such as "violet-shy" or *veilchenscheu* is syntactically but not semantically acceptable here. In this case, the incomprehensible notion of "a dislike for violets" would be the likely interpretation of the compound. In the German version of the sentence given above, the translator has opted for a relative clause to convey the original meaning:

> *Emily? Klein – so diese Art Mädchen, die wie schüchterne Veilchen sind.*

> (Literally: Emily? Small – like the kind of girls who are like shy violets)

3.8 Symbolic Features

An additional complication in a Russian translation involves the symbolic notion of violets. According to native-speaker assessment, the flower "mimosa" (*мимоза*) would probably be used, signifying delicacy, sentimentalism, tenderness, etc.

The term "salt-burning", in another description of the encounter between the two protagonists in *The Rainbow*, has another type of complication in that contextual information is vital for interpretation:

> *If he could but net her brilliant, cold, **salt-burning** body in the soft iron of his own hands.*

The concept of salt is a reference by Lawrence to the pillar of Biblical salt when Lot's wife is change into a salt statue (Luke: 7). The metaphor corresponds to Jesus's reply to the Pharisees who ask when the kingdom of God will come. In this way, they would avoid returning to a former way of life in which they may spiritually be changed into a salt statue. Lawrence evokes the double image of the salt statue and the "burning haystacks" in the moonlight which matches Ursula's body.[17]

The translation of "salt-burning" into French incorporates this notion of salt with the literal simile, "corrosive like salt":

*Si seulement il pouvait enfermer son corps brillant, froid, et **corrosif comme le sel** dans ses douces mains de fer.*

However, the translation into German (1964), avoids the important association with salt, (literally: bitter singeing), even though the Biblical reference is in the same chapter:

*Er hätte gerne ihren funkelnden, **bitter versengenden** Leib mit dem schmiegsamen Netz seiner Hände umschlossen.*

The interesting point about the lack of reference to salt, or being unaware of the reference out of context, is that a number of other interpretations become possible in native-speaker assessment. The notion of salt is difficult to conceptualise in the compound and therefore avoided: e.g. ... *ihren strahlenden, kalten, brennenden Körper*... in German (her shining, cold, burning body) or *увядающее тело* (a withering body) on the analogy of putting salt on plants which make them fade and wither. It is at this point that contextual information is vital to estimate whether the same metaphoric images are accessible in each language.

The foregoing discussions illustrate the point that certain linguistic structures such as composites substantially enhance the atmosphere of literary discourse, but that the structures between languages vary considerably for syntactic, semantic or other reasons. In the search for the origins of figurative language, the words which can be read in a text therefore depend on the linguistic possibilities that a writer has available in the language of the literary work. Each language has its own morpho-syntactic, semantic and conceptual frameworks. This is revealed by the process of translation which demonstrates that it is not easy, and sometimes impossible, to transfer figurative innovation from one language to another. This also depends on the flexibility of poetic licence.

From a mono- and multilingual perspective, linguistic structures therefore represent the first layer of the six-tier model in the order outlined in the previous chapter. Lawrence's innovations, as well as those of other poets, are often difficult to re-convey in a foreign language using the same stylistic format. The conclusion from a contrastive linguistic approach is that the potential and the form of figurative invention in any language must depend partly on the lexical, semantic, phonological and morpho-syntactic structures available to the language concerned.

The figurative expressions created by Lawrence in the examples given above combine feelings of love within an austere environment. What mental processes are involved in these textual and stylistic patterns? The second step requires investigating theories on human thought in relation to the words chosen. The next chapter will therefore examine thought processes in the next layer down.

Notes

1 Whorf (1956).
2 Kövecses (2006: 34, 322).
3 Nunberg (2006).
4 Mayakovsky (1975).
5 Nikitina (2009: 1).
6 idem. Nikitina (2009: 6).
7 idem. Nikitina (2009:7).
8 Noch.' (ночь)/Nadevayete luchsheye platye.
9 Cazé (2007).
10 Chevalier and Gheerbrant (1969).
11 Bensimon (1990: 84).
12 Gouirand-Rousselon (2002).
13 Trim (2015: 93–106).
14 Translation from Günther (1964).
15 I am grateful to Ulrich von Kusserow and Angelika Richter for German examples.
16 I am grateful to Elena Kocheshkova for Russian examples.
17 Trim (2018b: 337).

4 Underlying Figurative Thought

4.1 Cross-Language Imagery

The preceding chapter suggested that, by comparing languages, linguistic structure probably plays a part in how we think and write and what the potential of stylistic tools is. Further evidence on this issue, and equally related to cross-language issues, is provided by facts, which leave the domain of language structure and enter thought processes. At this second stage of investigating origins, the following example proposes that, in the case of German and Spanish, the gender of nouns can influence the way speakers symbolise a given set of concepts.[1] Syntax may thus play a role in language-specific conceptualisation.

On the basis of an experiment involving the word "key", informants in an experiment created "masculine" adjectives for nouns with masculine gender and vice versa for female gender. Participants thought of related attributes such as "heavy", "jagged" or "serrated" for the masculine gender of *der Schlüssel* in German and different symbols such as "golden", "intricate" and "little" for the feminine gender of Spanish *la clave*. The reverse occurred for opposite genders between the languages which involved the word "bridge". The feminine gender of German *die Brücke* evoked elegance, fragility and peace according to the results of the experiment, while the masculine gender of Spanish *el puente* symbolized danger, strength and length. Whatever the level of influence played by language structure on thought processes, a contrastive linguistic approach implies some important features in conceptualisation. In the same way as language influences stylistic force, it seems to influence, to a certain extent, the perception of the environment.

DOI: 10.4324/9781032130378-4

In line with the Whorfian hypotheses mentioned in the previous chapter, the limitations of linguistic influence on thought are, nevertheless, speculative and a perusal of the cultural history of many symbols can leave a great deal of questions unanswered. If Lawrence's symbol of the moon is again taken into consideration, a breakdown of its major links to masculine/feminine divinity reveals substantial diversity. According to Chevalier and Gheerbrant,[2] the moon has generally been associated with feminine qualities across cultures. One of the reasons is that it often has a marital link to its masculine counterpart of the sun. At some point in the history of the Inca civilisation in South America, the moon was the wife of the sun and the stars were their children.[3] However, this is not always the case. Taking the example of South America regarding the American Indian *Ge* tribe of Brazil, the moon is a masculine divinity without any association with the sun.

Some environmental and cultural factors may provide answers to these differences. Apparently, the moon is traditionally masculine in the Arab world, while the sun is feminine. One of the reasons given is that the night is cooler and therefore a better time for travelling with regard to nomadic tribes. Presumably, patriarchal reasoning, as in most traditional cultures, would enter this debate. Whatever the specific traits and possible reasons may be, variation appears to be considerable in cultural history.

As far as European languages and culture are concerned, the same variation appears to be predominant in the morpho-syntax of the moon and the sun. In Old English, the moon (*móna*) was a masculine noun,[4] in line with present-day Germanic languages such as German *der Mond*. However, the moon is traditionally feminine in the Latinate languages as in Latin *luna* and its correspondences in present-day Romance languages. Although English lost its gender in inanimate noun classes, the masculine form has been retained in a language such as German. Such stability is not reflected in the Germanic gender of the sun. This arbitrary relationship between language structure and conceptualisation requires additional tools. A useful and practical framework can be found in cognition.

4.2 Cognitive Theories

Ideas on the modern term of cognitive psychology, as a science of the human mind, go back to the time of Plato who felt that the brain was the centre of mental processes. Much later, ideas revolved around the concepts of empiricism[5] (John Locke) and nativism (Immanuel Kant).

In the first half of the 20th century, the American school of behaviourism played a major role in psychology,[6] the claim being that human thoughts and feelings are subject to controlling variables in behaviour. It therefore suggests that language productivity is based on the learning of activities and events in the environment. This was rejected by Chomsky's generative approach to syntax[7] which maintained that an infinite number of language structures could be created in the mind, independent of the imitation patterns of behaviourism.

There has been a controversial debate in the past on what constitutes cognition. Chomsky is the linguist who is often quoted as representing the cognitive turn of direction in the history of cognitive psychology. In linguistics, however, it has been suggested that the label "cognitive" cannot be applied to Chomskyan linguistics. One claim is that:

> The classical position, and the one required by the mathematics used in generative linguistics, is that a category is defined by necessary and sufficient conditions. But empirical research in the various cognitive sciences has shown that this is grossly incorrect for real categories; instead, the human category system is based on basic-level and prototype-centered categories of various kinds – graded, metonymic, and radial (...) Thus, the Cognitive Commitment is at odds with the Chomskyan Commitment.[8]

It appears that the criticism also entails the limitation of defining mathematical conditions for linguistic productivity, while ignoring the type of flexibility seen in features such as prototype-centred categories.[9] These suggest that there are more typical types of relevant images at the centre of a conceptual category and that they become less typical towards the outer limits. Despite some basic differences in the two arguments put forward, there are common links. Both approaches suggest that the mind itself is creative and, although the results are claimed to be different, they contribute to an infinite form of productivity. If individual psychology is taken into account, and this must be a fundamental point in cognition itself, it is likely that variation in figurative language takes on an infinite structure similar to Chomsky's generative approach to syntax. Prototype-centred categories clearly support the idea of flexibility and, particularly in the case of literary discourse, suggest that non-conventional figurative ideas are boundless. At the same time, the fact that typical images are found at the centre of prototype categories and become less typical towards the edge equally suggests that there are limits in figurative innovation. If a mapping extends beyond the boundary, it is likely that a figure of speech would not be understood or be simply nonsensical.

At this point, it should be mentioned that, in accordance with cross-cultural conceptualisation, boundaries may be moved. A particular symbol in one language may not be understood in another, or only partially, so that the boundaries of categorisation and their corresponding mappings also move according to the culture involved. The same applies to all kinds of figures of speech such as idiomatic expressions. They may have some of the signs or symbols to be found in an equivalent idiom in another language. Equally, a completely different idiom in another language might be understood due to overlapping cultural conceptualisation or, on the contrary, entirely misunderstood if the prototype categories do not fit cross-linguistically.

4.3 Individual Conceptualisation

It would appear, however, that the extremely wide variation of conceptualisation possible in the human mind generally contributes to the highly personalised creativity found in discourse. The roots of individual conceptualisation have also been analysed differently according to varied schools of psychology between countries or continents. A typical cleavage can be seen between the American cognitive school and the European Freudian approaches. The latter may help to explain certain figurative imagery in 20th century European literature. Since the Freudian approach, in particular, is concerned with individual psychology rather than the more universal types of cognitive linguistic models outlined below, it would be useful to emphasise this particular point in the following example.

The poetry of Sylvia Plath has been the subject of a great deal of debate with regard to child/parent relationships and particularly the ambiguity about whether her father or mother is the topic of her works. However, the poem *Medusa* clearly reflects her relationship with her mother from whom she wished to break ties. It has been suggested that it invokes two meanings: its mythological application and Plath's reference to the stinging, negative effects of a "jellyfish" which are associated to an overbearing mother in the content of the poem.[10]

> Did I escape, I wonder?
> My mind winds to you
> Old barnacled umbilicus, Atlantic cable,
> Keeping itself, it seems, in a state of miraculous repair.

34 Underlying Figurative Thought

A Freudian approach to analysing the representation of Plath's mother as a jellyfish would involve the Oedipus complex. This implies hatred for the same-sex parent. Although Sylvia Plath was close to her mother, these feelings appear in the poem with images such as "old barnacled umbilicus", likened to an underwater telephone cable linking her to her mother on the other side of the Atlantic.

In the search into the origins of figurative language, an overview of the relevant literature reveals that the focus on metaphor, in particular, has been the subject of study since time immemorial. In fact, metaphor studies have gone through many different approaches since Aristotle and beyond. To name just a few more recent ones in 20th century American research: the comparison theory defines metaphoric labels such as the "tenor" (what is being said) and the "vehicle" (the way of saying it).[11] The interactionist view, linked to the comparison theory, places equal emphasis on both similarity and dissimilarity regarding the source and target domains of mapping.[12] A more extreme approach to metaphor, among others, is the anomaly view[13] which claims that metaphor is viewed as a mistake or absurdity since it conflicts with literal meaning.

4.4 Cognitive Linguistics

A more recent approach, and which will be adopted in the following discussions, is a cognitive linguistic one. In particular, it raises the question of figurative thought behind linguistic expressions. What is going on in the mind when a figurative expression is created? This view of metaphor, which started in the 1980s, has been widely reported in the literature. Just one or two of the relevant aspects will be selected here for the purpose of tracing origins in the types of examples discussed. In general, it takes into consideration physiological and environmental conceptualisation with regard to feelings and concepts. As far as the language/thought interface is concerned, one of the analytical tools in cognitive linguistics adopts a basic theory: explanations of the images used in cognitive metaphor require a contrast being made between the expression created in a language and the underlying figurative mapping which corresponds to it. This distinction has been highlighted, above all, in cognitive metaphor theory, or CMT.[14]

The distinction is fundamental since numerous examples in language can be grouped together under one base mapping expressed in thought, albeit with a certain degree of interpretation in some cases, and projected onto its subsequent creations in language. The name given to the equation in the base mapping may therefore be relatively flexible, but it serves the practical purpose of defining the overall thought process. The language category will be termed here *linguistic metaphor* and the thought category *conceptual metaphor*. The latter thereby involves a mapping in thought which may be extrapolated from the linguistic expression. In this way, a typical example of a linguistic metaphor in this field, "our marriage has been a long bumpy road", is mapped from a LOVE IS A JOURNEY conceptual metaphor.[15] This is similar to the LIFE IS A JOURNEY metaphor raised in the discussion of poetry in chapter 1.

Two basic examples of this theory are hypotheses arising from the early work on CMT. The types of conceptual metaphors formulated can be seen in some very basic examples. One is that the conceptualisation of the environment is often founded on a theory termed the *Spatialisation of Form Hypothesis*.[16] This implies, for example, that POSITIVE IS UPWARDS and NEGATIVE IS DOWN, according to spatial orientation. The second example is that the environment is often viewed in terms of basic properties such as lightness and darkness: POSITIVE IS LIGHT and NEGATIVE IS DARK.[17] The values and qualities on the left-hand side of the equation are mapped onto concepts on the right-hand side. A quote from the novel *The Rainbow*, "as if she had drunk strong, glowing sunshine", is therefore a positive metaphor based on light. Other basic concepts and human activities or experience are also integrated into this form of conceptualisation, although certain concepts may be subject to cultural symbolism. A flower, such as a rose, would usually be positive, while a toxic substance in the form of poison would logically be negative.

4.5 Metaphor and Symbol

These processes are therefore linked to a base mapping from a source to target domain in figures of speech such as metaphor and symbolism. Some figures of speech entail others and often in multiple form. They include symbols containing several metaphors. It has been suggested in the cognitive linguistic literature that cultural symbols, in particular, may be based on well-entrenched metaphors in culture. A common symbol of life, for example, is the concept of fire. The latter is used as a metaphor of life and can be seen in linguistic expressions such as "to snuff out someone's life". A typical symbol of a culture can be seen in the Statue of Liberty in New York. There are a number of cultural ideas, such as knowledge, liberty and justice, which are depicted in this particular statue. They include, for example, the bearing of a torch symbolising knowledge.[18]

Multiple images can also be seen in metaphors and, in particular, compound structures described in the previous chapters. It was seen that Lawrence not only uses a lot of creative metaphors in his writing, he joins two or more ideas or images into the same compound word. Cognitively speaking, the reading of a single-image metaphor already evokes two images since, particularly in the case of creative language, the source and target concepts come to mind at the same time. A compound metaphor thereby evokes three or more images automatically: two from the source and at least one in the target domain. The term "salt-burning" thus contains the two source images of salt and fire mapped onto the image of Ursula's body, according to the interpretation envisaged by the author. As in the notion of blends,[19] two images are merged together in metaphor. It would appear that compounds thereby merge multiple images into what becomes, in effect, a blended concept within one metaphor.

This would arguably constitute a basic difference in language structure between expressions in the forms of metaphors and similes. An additional claim here is that the use of a simile has a different stylistic result. By using the expression, "X is like Y", the two images X and Y become separated, rather than being conceptualised as the same blend. The end result is that one metaphoric lexeme is seen as one concept, albeit mixed, whereas a simile is a phrase which presents two images side by side. Consequently, it may be hypothesised here that the one-lexeme construction, as mentioned in the preceding chapter, contributes to the stylistically more powerful figure of speech seen in Lawrence's innovations. This force would be lost in a simile.

Throughout the amorous encounters in *The Rainbow*, the different morpho-syntactic examples reveal new features when combined with cognitive theories and, in particular, cognitive stylistics. This relatively recent field is associated with mind style[20] in combination with metaphor studies.[21] A mind style has been defined as "any distinctive linguistic representation of an individual mental self",[22] and the reference here is to the fictional world. It has been suggested that "studies on mind style in fiction have shown how different linguistic phenomena such as lexical choice, syntactic patterns and transitivity can be used to project a narrator's or character's idiosyncratic perception of the world".[23] Consequently, these views also suggest that in the novel, *One Flew over the Cuckoo's Nest,*[24] for example, the narrator Bromden's mind style is based on a number of conventional conceptual metaphors such as PEOPLE ARE MACHINES. The conventional metaphors are used in creative ways which may not only be standard but also innovative or 'deviant'. Although this novel deals with 'deviant' forms of thought in mental illness, it has been emphasised that the notion of mind style in language generally should include standard forms.[25]

The innovative style is characteristic of the original English version of this novel. It has equally been proposed that an exact imitation of the source language's style is difficult in translation, particularly with regard to features such as idiomaticity. This has been pointed out in relation to its translation into the Dutch language. To maintain stylistic coherence in translation: "changing the metaphor here means changing the mind style. And changing the mind style means changing the narrative world".[26] If this is the case, it would support the argument in the preceding chapter that each language has its own lexical, syntactic and stylistic models available to the writer using the language in question, and that these models cannot always be imitated from one language to the next.

It will be proposed here that, in line with a cognitive linguistic framework, the scenes in Lawrence's examples reflect a generalised LOVE IS DEATH conceptual metaphor throughout the novel in which the concept of love implies an "impossible love" situation. The narrative framework is thus directed towards an overall *mortality scenario* concerning emotions and feelings in which love is mapped onto death. In other words, the symbol of death reflects this particular kind of love and the relationship is doomed. Images in "saltburning", such as Biblical salt and fire mapped onto a lover's body, imply that love is unattainable or cannot be fulfilled. Lawrence's lexical and syntactic choice could therefore be seen as the narrator's own idiosyncratic perception of the world at that time and therefore his particular mind style.

In CMT, there are many mappings of love, but none appear to have this specific mapping with death. Some basic ones can be seen in the following:[27]

LOVE IS A NUTRIENT:	I am *starved* for love
LOVE IS WAR:	She *conquered* him
LOVE IS A PHYSICAL FORCE:	I was *magnetically drawn* to her
LOVE IS FIRE:	I am *burning* with love

In recent years, however, CMT has not been without criticism regarding gaps in the overall picture. The following debate will look at one particular problem area regarding such criticism: the difference between everyday language and literary metaphor. The standard CMT model does not tend to make a distinction between the two, particularly in the case of origins, since it is argued that literary texts use the same conventional conceptual metaphors as everyday discourse. This argument is supported by the fact that literary discourse simply extends, elaborates, combines or contrasts them in novel ways.[28] In other words, the two types of discourse are not considered to be different disciplines and standard CMT suggests that poetic metaphor involves a non-automatic cognitive process in contrast to everyday language.

Throughout the history of European schools of thought regarding linguistics and literature, cooperation between the two has fluctuated considerably for various reasons. One particular example has concerned differing viewpoints in stylistics, as in classical rhetoric and grammar, from the 19th century onwards. This came to a head during the structuralist period.[29] More recently, it has been suggested that CMT presents two particular problems for literary analysis. The first is that CMT involves a more universal and reductionist approach compared to more detailed textual analysis in literature. The second, and particularly with regard to metaphor origins, is that the study of figurative language in literature focuses more specifically on an author's individual creativity and therefore on literary ingenuity.[30]

4.6 Cognitive and Conflictual Paradigms

The cohabitation of the disciplines of linguistics and literature has undoubtedly been a difficult one, and many volumes could be written on the subject. Conflictual viewpoints can, of course, be seen within each discipline. In the case of linguistics, one recent idea will be taken up here with regard to what will be termed *cognitive and conflictual paradigms*. The first refers to CMT and the second to conflicts in conceptualisation (not disciplinary conflicts). However, they also involve everyday and literary distinctions. As has been pointed out, a reconciliatory approach in disciplinary conflicts is "not to highlight one model to the detriment of the other, but to identify the limits of each and to find a proper place for both within a comprehensive view".[31]

It has been proposed that there are many types of figures of speech and that they all have different grammatical, conceptual and semantic properties. For this reason, it would appear contradictory to the CMT idea that "metaphor means metaphorical concept",[32] i.e. the covert supposition that metaphor exists in a singular form.[33] On this basis, the conflictual paradigm highlights the importance of syntax and suggests that this component of language begins when atomic meanings are connected in unexpected and creative ways: "unlike words, syntactic constructions do not simply carry meanings: they put meanings together in potentially creative ways. This is the point at which the observation of conflictual complex meanings becomes relevant".[34]

In this light, the conflictual paradigm is opposed to the idea that CMT makes no difference between conventional and "living metaphors"[35] since it claims that both originate in the same underlying metaphorical concepts. The conflictual approach suggests that the dividing line between conventional and living figures is sometimes difficult to draw since it depends on the presence or absence of conceptual conflict. However, conventional figures tend to be based on a shared heritage, as in the conceptual metaphor TIME IS MONEY, whereas the second represents a conceptual conflict as it challenges shared conceptual structures. In the example, "and Winter pours its grief in snow" from the writing of Emily Brontë, grief is not the kind of substance we can pour. This quote would therefore represent a living metaphor whose content is not contained in the sense of a word but in the complex interpretations of a whole sentence.

In short, there is an ongoing debate about differences between shared conceptual structures in everyday language and more innovative expressions in literary discourse. This would therefore have an impact on the origins of figurative language since the first would involve drawing on shared conceptualisation and the second on the ability to innovate within the linguistic and conceptual structures of the language being used. Poetic licence would thus be confined to the limits of interpretation in the language with the risk of being misunderstood if the limits are crossed.

The end result is that literary discourse undoubtedly contains both conventional and living metaphors whose boundary is indeed difficult to define. However, the preceding discussion reveals that the tracing of origins in figurative language, whether it be shared or innovative features, also requires additional information than simply mapping an image from a source to target domain. Amongst this information, cultural and textual or contextual information is also required. Some of these issues have been addressed since the early days of CMT in the 1980s.

With regard to the first feature of culture, a major question which comes to the fore is the extent to which people around the world share their understandings of aspects of the world in which they live.[36] One example is: "love is like a wagon – we both have a responsibility for pulling it along". In CMT, this not only implies the culture-based notion of COLLABORATIVE WORK but also images such as

40 Underlying Figurative Thought

'wagon'. It involves cultural activities of transport or work according to the geographical place and time involved. Indeed, it represents a basic issue whose importance has been raised not only in cross-cultural studies but also in historical linguistics.[37] Culture often determines long-term paths of figurative thought and may also be the reason for the way figures of speech are structured, as opposed to other factors such physiological influences.

The second feature of context is also equally important in the interpretation of mappings. One suggestion is that "context is never predetermined and objectively existing; it must be created (and re-created) in the course of the communicative process (...) Meaning construction is a dynamic and creative process that results from the interaction of (more or less) conventional meanings (...) based on embodied experience, on the one hand, and the contextual factors deemed to be relevant, on the other".[38] Without contextual information, very many figurative structures are undoubtedly impossible to interpret in many types of language.

A cognitive approach in the CMT model has therefore evolved from studies on purely source to target domain mappings, which indicate what types of images are used, to the incorporation of other vital parameters such as culture and context. In many cases, individual items are either based on one predominant feature or are a mixture of several, including aspects such as individual psychological experience and the psychoanalysis of life history.[39]

It can be seen from this discussion that, apart from the vital inclusion of other parameters such culture and context, the controversy about language structure is an important one and has a much larger part to play in other approaches to figurative language than CMT. The "living metaphors" and "conceptual conflict" theories are in this category and strengthen the debate on innovative language structures in literature and the more conventional models found in everyday language.

Other recent approaches which highlight language structure include *Mediationism Theory* in French linguistics (from the French '*médiationnisme*').[40] This incorporates factors such as culture and history. Mediationism tends to reject the more mentalist CMT approach by stating that language structure is vital in the transmission of ideas through the centuries. Its focus is on linguistic signs and thereby on linguistic history and socio-cultural characteristics. The claim is that ideas are a fundamental part of language itself.

It can be seen from this chapter that there have been many approaches to the study of figurative thought. At the present time, a very useful analytical tool appears to be the framework of cognitive linguistics which, however, can have certain weaknesses in the analysis of literary discourse. At the same time, the distinction between conceptual and linguistic metaphor is fundamental and represents an excellent way in analysing literary corpora. The cross-cultural approach adopted here also highlights the importance of taking culture into account when establishing conceptual metaphor models.

In this light, the third step in the six-tier model will look at cultural history with applications and adaptations from the CMT point of view. The next chapter will examine how not only cultural history, but also its associated linguistic history, are mapped onto conceptual models.

Notes

1 Boroditsky et al. (2003).
2 Chevalier and Gheerbrant (1969: 589ff).
3 idem. Chevalier and Gheerbrant (1969), citing Means (1931).
4 Bessinger (1977: 45).
5 Locke [1689] (1988).
6 Skinner (1938).
7 Chomsky (1957).
8 Lakoff (1991: 54).
9 Originally developed by Rosch (1975).
10 Cited by Kövecses (2015: 127).
11 Richards (1965).
12 idem. Richards (1965).
13 Harris (1976).
14 Lakoff and Johnson (1980).
15 Gibbs (1994: 148ff.), citing op. cit. Lakoff and Johnson (1980).
16 Lakoff (1987: 283).
17 idem. Lakoff (1987: 271).
18 Kövecses (2005).
19 Fauconnier and Turner (2003).
20 Fowler (1977).
21 Semino (2007); Semino and Swindlehurst (1996).
22 Op. cit. Fowler (1977: 103).
23 Dorst (2019).
24 Kesey (1962).
25 Pillière (2013: 7).
26 Op. cit. Dorst (2019).
27 Kövecses (2000: 26).
28 Lakoff and Turner (1989); Dorst (2019).
29 Maingueneau (2002).
30 Fludernik (2011).

31 Prandi (2017).
32 Op. cit. Lakoff and Johnson (1980).
33 Prandi (2017: 6).
34 idem. Prandi (2017: 33).
35 A term used by Ricoeur [1975] (1978).
36 Op. cit. Kövecses (2005: 2).
37 Trim (2011).
38 Kövecses (2015: 71ff).
39 idem. Kövecses (2015), citing Borebely (1998).
40 Nyckees (2007: 2).

5 Tracing Cultural History

5.1 Diachronic Conceptual Networking

To what extent are figurative words and thoughts new or old? Some types of metaphors and symbols are undoubtedly innovative and personalised. However, it is rare to come across a word or idea which is entirely new, even if the most obscure type of neologism is used. As has been pointed out, the creative expression has to fit into the language and culture in which an author is writing, otherwise it would make no sense. It is true that some themes, such as love, are more universal and have existed since time immemorial. Others, like metaphors based on internet technology and social networks, are much newer. However, all require a well-defined linguistic and conceptual framework in order to be understood.

One major feature within the historical evolution of figurative language, which a writer accesses in reproducing either conventional or innovative expressions, is a process termed *diachronic conceptual networking*.[1] This is particularly the case in metaphor evolution. It suggests there are regular patterns of conceptualisation which evolve through the centuries and are linked to preceding conceptual structures. Many universal images of basic concepts in standard CMT, such as flat, smooth, tight, loose, dry, wet, cold, fire, and so on, have been used for the same figurative concepts for centuries. They are founded on "building blocks", which often represented conceptual metaphors a long time ago. The LOVE IS HEAT/FIRE metaphor, for example, can be traced back to Ovid's *Metamophosis: ignes ipse suos nutrit* (feeds the fire that burns him) or Petrarch's *Il Canzioniere: si che 'l foco di Giove in parte spense* (so that Jove's fire was quenched a little).[2]

Associated with these long-term patterns, a considerable degree of variation can occur diachronically: certain items may become dormant during specific periods and re-activated at different times later on. Furthermore, many conceptual metaphors are subject to variational polysemy through time: words add and lose meanings as the centuries pass by. To add to this, variation may concern the diachronic salience of expressions: some figurative senses may be used more frequently by a language community at a particular time in history. This particular aspect may affect the comprehension and interpretation of metaphors. All such types of variation, when compared both synchronically and diachronically across different languages and cultures, become even more extensive. Historical change can also have an impact on both language structure and semantic evolution. Finally, variation occurs between the type of conventionalised metaphor discussed above and literary innovation.

To give a brief overview of some of these patterns, a number of examples will be cited. Within the theme of love, the LOVE IS FIRE conceptual metaphor can be seen to be long-term. Conventional expressions such as "a burning passion" are linked to this base mapping, whereas innovative metaphors like 'salt-burning' involve "living metaphors" or "conceptual conflict" in the previous chapter. The conventional image of heat in the body, linked to passion, has become conventional and is a part of cultural heritage, whereas the act or state of burning salt is not the case.

The LOVE IS MONEY theme is a common mapping today in expressions such as "money can't buy you love", but it was not the case in the Middle Ages. The financial side of metaphors will be taken up below. However, it could be said that the medieval love/money equation was therefore less salient during the medieval period. Love was usually equated with noble causes such as courtly love in literature, although there were exceptions in the humorous tales written by authors like Boccacio and Chaucer. One of these exceptions in the literary works of that time involved secular attitudes in Chaucer's *The Wife of Bath*. This tale used the financial theme in marriage and physical love for comic effect: *For as a spaynel she wol on him lepe til that she finde som man hir to chepe* (For she will leap on him like a spaniel until she finds some man who will buy her wares).[3] A number of possible explanations have been given for this rather exceptional situation, particularly as it was in the words of a woman: the Wife of Bath was perhaps "a female representative of the upwardly mobile mercantile class" created by Chaucer to communicate some of his views on the matter.[4] The debate in literary criticism on this issue has been an extensive one since *The Canterbury Tales* are open to a great deal of interpretation. The theme of marital harmony may have reflected Chaucer's own feelings, and he may have been "ahead of his time" in this respect.[5]

5.2 Diachronic Salience

A writer's thoughts may therefore influence the salience of figurative language at a given time, in the same way as varying concerns can become predominant with social, political or philosophical changes. Such concerns today can involve, for example, ecology and global warming. Changing ideas in history, often depending on the country and culture, are therefore responsible for either fluctuating salience or dormant versus active figures of speech in discourse.

Certain metaphors concerning religion, for example, have decreased steadily in American literature since the 17th century.[6] Possible explanations may be found in the evolution of social and religious life in North America. The writers Matthews, Bradstreet, Edwards and Franklin dealt with religious issues in the areas of Boston and Philadelphia during the 17th and 18th centuries. On the other hand, writers of the 19th and 20th centuries, such as Cooper, Emerson, Twain and Hemingway, tended to focus more on man and his environment. The reason for this is no doubt the fact that the opening up of the Far West required the need to confront the hardships of extreme environmental conditions at that time.

The financial aspect, mentioned above, of metaphor mapping in English has increased sharply since the Industrial Revolution. There are very many conventional expressions such as "I'll buy that" (to agree). The rise of the capitalist era appears to be a major cause. One theory for this in metaphor studies is linked to the notion of "hidden ideologies".[7] It suggests that there are latent ideologies in our way of thinking that are the result of the ways in which ready-made categorisations of ontologies are handed down through the generations. These ideologies are subconscious and become normalised in our thoughts. The origins can be found in economic philosophers such as Thomas Hobbes, David Hume, Robert Malthus and Adam Smith. The main tenets of this philosophy is found in two strands of thinking: the first is that humans, like animals, are basically competitive and extend their interests only to the family and close friends; the second is that quality is expressed as quantity and that all human values such as well-being, relationships, time and even virtue are reflected in money or material possessions.[8]

5.3 Historical Origins of Figurative Words

The theories discussed so far concern mainly ideas in society during different historical periods. They have an effect on features such as conceptual metaphors or symbolism according to the cultural environment. The actual words or expressions used in any given language tend to be more complex with regard to their patterns of evolution. Tracing the origins of words with figurative meanings can be complex due to changing polysemy and synonymy. This complicates the history of linguistic signs as bearers of culture since one word may be associated with any number of meanings at one time and vice versa.

In poetry and other literary discourse, however, the choice of words is important. A writer may choose a specific word for its particularly evocative nature. Lawrence's innovation "flame-lurid" arguably contains the evocative word of "lurid". This literally came to mean, among other concepts, "shining with a red glare", originally from Latin *luridus*, and took on the meanings of "ominous" and "ghastly" in the 19th century[9]. This would therefore fit in very well to describing the scene in his novel *Annie and Frank* discussed above. Over a longer period of time, diachronic polysemy/synonymy becomes more complex due to transformation of linguistic signs according to existing lexical or morpho-syntactic rules in a language or borrowing, as well as semantic extension and loss or metaphorisation. A brief look at the word "shield" demonstrates this point.

From a figurative point of view, a glance at any English dictionary will reveal that a conventional conceptual metaphor of this item would be PROTECTION IS A SHIELD.[10] Hence, there are expressions such as "insurance is a shield against disaster".[11] This notion has been extended to US military campaign code names in the modern day such as "Liberty Shield" during the second military intervention in Iraq (2003). Historically, the conceptual metaphor has had the meaning of "preparing for war". In Old English, the raising of shields among soldiers symbolised this movement:

> Then in the great hall hard blades were drawn
>
> swords above benches, many broad shields
>
> raised high in hand[12]

Beowulf, ll. 1288–1290

The "preparing for war/conflict" meaning in the raising of shields is a part of European culture. It was used in the Crusades and today it varies across languages: in modern-day French, it is used in the field of social unrest and is similar to the modern English expression "to be up in arms about something".[13]

The fluctuating meaning of this term can be seen more clearly in the idea of protection by a large organisation. In this case, the actual word is different, using *aegis* of Greek origin, as in 'under the aegis of...'. During the course of history, the word for the concept of shield has also fluctuated in English. In *Beowulf*, there was an alternation between Old English *scyld* and *rand*. These terms often had the connotation of weapons using magical powers. As a result, the changing patterns between a word and meaning in figurative language, in contrast to more regular patterns in the types of conceptual metaphors described above, are often complex and difficult to trace back over a long period of time. The choice of a specific word and its meaning in literary discourse may often be associated with relatively recent historical evolution.

5.4 The Love/Death Conceptual Metaphor

With regard to the conceptual metaphor pattern, one mapping, which appears to be culturally and historically widespread in literature, is LOVE IS DEATH. Although apparently innovative in the CMT terms of everyday language, this mapping has a long literary history for very specific reasons. The close relationship between love and death has been highlighted throughout the history of European literature in the examples of *Tristan & Isolde* and the death wish in Wagner's opera, *Tristan*. Another example of the long-term aspect can be seen in Shakespearean plays and parallel situations in Greek tragedies. The suicide scenes in *Romeo and Juliet* and *Antony and Cleopatra* are reminiscent of the two lovers, Pyramus and Thisbe in Ovid's *Metamorphoses*.[14] In this tale, the two would meet at night near a mulberry tree but, one evening, Thisbe arrived and fled on seeing a lioness approaching her. With her blood-stained paws after hunting, the lioness mauled Thisbe's cloak which she had dropped. Soon afterwards, Pyramus arrived on the scene and, fearing the worst after seeing the blood-stained cloak, stabbed himself. This is therefore a very early suicide scene in literature involving love.[15]

It has been claimed that there are some essential differences between Shakespeare's plays and Greek tragedies. One example is that the horrors of a funeral scene in Shakespearean literature tend to reinforce the ardour of a lover, contrary to Ancient Greek plays.[16] This can be seen in *Romeo & Juliet*[17]:

> That unsubstantial Death is amorous, bodiless Death is your lover
>
> And that the lean abhorrèd monster keeps horrible
>
> Thee here in dark to be his paramour mistress[18]

The personification of death as a lover and the monster, who refers to Romeo's rival, Paris, whom he has just killed and placed in Juliet's tomb, reinforces the horror of the death scene. Likewise, the symbol of worms being chambermaids reinforces Romeo's wish to remain with his lover, despite the horror of them eating into her body:

> Here, here will I remain
>
> With worms that are thy chambermaids. O, here
>
> Will I set up my everlasting rest[19]

It could be suggested here that the underlying conceptual metaphor of the LOVE IS DEATH mapping may actually reinforce aspects in a relationship such as commitment to love. This can be seen in the notion of being wedded in death by using a bridegroom metaphor in *Antony & Cleopatra*:

> But I will be
>
> A bridegroom in my death, and run into't
>
> As to a lover's bed.[20]

Secondary mappings from the LOVE IS DEATH metaphor can be extracted from Shakespeare's play such as:

LOVE IS BODILESS DEATH

LOVE ARE WORMS (ALIAS CHAMBERMAIDS)

LOVE IS A BRIDEGROOM IN DEATH

Behind the conceptual metaphors, it can also be assumed from this kind of data that the association of dying for the love of someone is an act of nobility, courage or esteem which is deeply rooted in European cultural history. However, this positive attitude to the mapping is only one of many forms and it can naturally be associated with negative values. In more modern comparative literature, this has been the case for a number of different reasons which can be gleaned from the context of various literary works.

Returning to linguistic history and the difficulty in tracing origins of figurative words as in the "shield" example given above, one major diachronic trend in the English language is the compounding of innovations as in Lawrence's creations. A breakdown of semantic units in the morphemes of composite patterns can sometimes help in comprehension such as in the language learning of long words formed in agglutinative languages like German and Russian. However, compounding may not always help in interpretation. It is a common feature in Shakespeare's language, and comprehension undoubtedly depends on whether a single lexeme in the compound is recognisable or not. This would apply to both foreign and early languages. One common morphological structure in Shakespeare is the noun + gerund combination as in the following example:

Till o'er their brows **death-counterfeiting sleep**

With leaden legs and batty wings doth creep.
(*Midsummer's Night Dream*: Act III, ii: 375–378)

A modern collocation would be to 'counterfeit money' with the basic sense of "to reproduce, imitate, etc.". The Shakespearean metaphor of 'death-counterfeiting' has been used to map sleep onto death in a similar way to the imagery of death discussed in the preceding chapter. The morphological structure has been used to figuratively collocate the imitation of death with sleep. In the same vein, the noun + gerund structure is used in the 'love-devouring death' metaphor in the following passage:

Do thou but close our hands with holy words, if you'll just join our hands

Then **love-devouring death** do what he dare.

It is enough I may but call her mine
(*Romeo & Juliet*: Act II,vi: 6–8)

The underlying personification of LOVE IS DEATH can be seen in the morphological derivation of "love-devouring", which succinctly combines the different images into one unit of adjective + noun. These compound adjectives are relatively easy to understand in the modern age. Others may be more complex since they are time-specific within the standard language of Early Modern English. They may also have particular attributes common to Shakespeare's personal innovations.

A reading of the following passage from the play *Much Ado About Nothing* reveals certain expressions which reveal difficulties of this kind. The scene is about the Beatrice's uncle, Leonato, who teases her about being matched with a fitting husband. Beatrice resists all such comments by referring in comic way with innovative figurative expressions to men in general:

Leonato: Well, niece, I hope to see you one day fitted with a husband.
Beatrice: Not till God make men of some other metal than earth.

Would it not grieve a woman to be overmaster'd with a pierce of

valiant dust? to make an account of her life to **a clod of wayward**

marl? No, uncle, I'll none: Adam's sons are my brethren, and

truly I hold it a sin to match in my kinred.
(*Much Ado About Nothing Act II, i: 57–65*)

The expression "valiant dust" seems less pejorative than "a clod of wayward marl", since it contains the word 'valiant', but it appears ironic combined with the word "dust". In the second expression, "wayward" could have a number of different meanings, but they are usually related to the senses of "capricious" and "unpredictable".[21] 'Marl', in the sense of 'clay', is again pejorative as in the image of 'dust'.

The words themselves are not new but reflect innovative collocations whose meanings may also vary according to the historical period. The term "valiant" in Shakespeare's time had the sense of "worthy, fine, hearty",[22] whereas today's meaning of this attribute tends towards the connotation of "brave, courageous, heroic, bold, etc.".[23] This passage could therefore reflect a scene in which the opposing values of the words in a collocation heighten the comic effect, although the stylistics may vary according to semantic change.

5.5 Understanding Figurative Language in Early Modern English

Symbolism in Shakespeare's language can become more complex and difficult to interpret if a large number of typical metaphoric expressions of the period are used in a passage. Without background knowledge to such symbols, a whole scene in this period of Early Modern English may become unclear or certain connotations in the passage remain incomprehensible. Again, the actual origin of certain anecdotes or meanings may not be known. The following scene, taken from *The Merry Wives of Windsor*, highlights this point:

Mrs Ford: Sir John? Art thou there, my **deer**? My male deer?
Fallstaff: My **doe** with the black scut? – Let the sky **rain potatoes**; let it thunder to the tune of *Green Sleeves*; hail **kissing-comfits** and **snow eryngoes**; let there come a tempest of provocation, I will shelter me here. (*Embracing her*)
(*The Merry Wives of Windsor, Act V, v*)

The origin of the symbolic metonym represented by the expression 'kissing-comfits' has been attributed by some dictionaries to Shakespeare's personal creation.[24] The meaning of this expression refers to sugar-plums, which are eaten to make the breath smell sweet. Etymologically, the term 'comfit' comes from Old French, and originally from Latin *conficere*, (to produce or to prepare). From a cognitive point of view, it can be seen that there are several levels of reference implied in this term. The first is a comparison between kissing and the sugar-plum. By eating the comfits, you are prepared for kissing: i.e. the conceptual metaphor of COMFITS ARE KISSING. At a deeper level, the reason why this mapping is possible is due to the fact that comfits produce sweet breath: SWEET BREATH IS KISSING. In other words, kisses are only possible (or desirable) with a sweet breath. The overall reason for including the metaphor in the passage is therefore one of seduction.

The term "eryngoes" refers to "a sweetmeat made from the candied root of the sea holly, deemed to be an aphrodisiac", and the reference to snow was probably the addition of sugar served with the candied root and which looked like snow. Furthermore, when potatoes were first introduced into England, they were also thought to be aphrodisiacs.²⁵ Hence, the different symbolic expressions of "raining potatoes", "kissing-comfits" and "snow eryngoes" all contribute to the scene of seduction. Each symbol is composed of a figurative structure, including the last one, in which the sugar coating is likened to snow.

Finally, the two protagonists in this scene refer to each other as a deer and a doe respectively, with the phonological play on the words 'deer' and 'dear', and there is likewise the symbolic reference to the Renaissance song, *Green Sleeves*. The lyrics to this song are about unrequited love, but the origins appear to be unclear, including many theories on the symbolic meanings of green. Some interpretations are associated with the concept of a "green gown", which dates back to the Middle Ages. One sense is that of a promiscuous woman due to the colouring of green on her clothes during love-play on grass.²⁶ There is also the popular legend that the song refers to Henry VIII's wooing of Anne Boleyn, although this seems unlikely,²⁷ particularly as the melody line is of Italian origin. All these aspects make the symbolic background to a passage difficult to fully comprehend. However, they all contribute to the cultural conceptualisation of figurative language at the time.

It can be seen that the word "kissing-comfits" has been compounded into one lexeme, which makes it a new word in its own right. Compounds can come in very many syntactic forms such as two nouns, an adjective and a noun, a gerund and a noun as in "kissing-comfits" and so on. As was seen in works by authors such as D. H. Lawrence, the English language lends itself well to this type of compounding due to its particular type of morphology. There is no doubt that this kind of morphological structure contributes a great deal to metaphorisation in English, and particularly in literary discourse. Sometimes the boundary between collocations and compounding can be very flexible but, at some point during the compilation of new words in dictionary entries, a word may be standardised in the form of a compound if a hyphen is added between the two morphemes. In other words, an expression such as "valiant dust" could be compounded into one word, "valiant-dust", which can sometimes attribute a different semantic and figurative status to the term. For example, the compound may become metonymic, whereas non-compounding might retain the sense of comparison as in a simile. Morphological derivation therefore introduces subtle varieties of interpretation.

The types of evolutionary processes in language and thought briefly described above show that, despite remarkable innovations in figurative language, they generally depend on what has existed before. Aspects may have been more or less salient at different times in history, but they all contribute to the ongoing evolution of language. For this reason, the diachronic dimension may reveal a considerable amount of information as to where words and ideas are coming from. Within an existing framework, personalised metaphorisation or symbolism can therefore subsequently develop in diverse and interesting ways.

Links to past cultural history thus supply important information as to how and why an author chooses certain words in his or her writing. However, more information about origins is often required than the sole analysis of words. This leads us onto the fourth stage of investigation into ultimate origins: the role of mapping context onto word meanings for a fuller interpretation of their use. A more precise feature of contextual information will be taken up here: the notion of reference. This aspect seems to have been largely neglected in more recent cognitive studies on conceptual mappings. The observation is particularly surprising since the topic has been studied in various linguistic and literary disciplines for a considerable period of time. Reference is a vital clue to why a mapping is used and, of course, to whom or what the mapping actually refers. From this point on, mappings will no longer be considered in isolation in the sense that the analysis is limited to which target domain images may be accessed by which source domain in a given culture and semantic field. The next chapter on reference will take up these vital clues in the continuing search for origins.

Notes

1 For a fuller discussion of this theory, see Trim (2007, Chapter 7).
2 For diachronic examples in the emotions, see Trim (2010: 223–260, 2011: 65ff).
3 Hieatt and Hieatt (1976: 194); Chaucer [c. 1400], *Wife of Bath's Tale,* ll. 267–268.
4 Dor (2003).
5 Howard (1960).
6 Smith et al. (1981).
7 Goatly (2007).
8 idem. Goatly (2007: 336).
9 Hoad (1987).
10 Op.cit. Trim (2011: 200ff).
11 Fowler and Fowler (1990).
12 *Beowulf,* 1288–1290. In Chickering (1977: 120–122).
13 Press title: Copenhagen – African countries raise their shields (*Copenhague – levée des boucliers des pays africains*; http://www.afrik.com/article1826.3.html).
14 Kenney (2008).
15 Ovid, *Metamorphoses,* Book 4, 55–166.

16 Girardin (1845).
17 I am grateful to Barrie Hesketh MBE for providing me with Shakespearian metaphor examples from his extensive databases.
18 *Romeo & Juliet*, Act 5, Scene 3.
19 idem. *Romeo & Juliet*, Act 5, Scene 3.
20 *Antony & Cleopatra*, Act 4, Scene 14, 99–101.
21 https://www.merriam-webster.com/ [accessed: 29/11/2018].
22 https://www.shakespeareswords.com/Public/Glossary.aspx?letter=k [accessed: 29/11/2018].
23 https://www.collinsdictionary.com/dictionary/english [accessed: 29/11/2018].
24 Op. cit. Merriam Webster.
25 Shipley (1984: 183–184).
26 Brown and McBride (2005: 1).
27 http://www.luminarium.org/renlit/greensleeves.htm/ [accessed: 29/11/2018].

6 Theories of Reference in Conceptual Mapping

6.1 Extra-Linguistic Reference

In any type of figurative mapping, the main question which arises from the word used is what or whom are we talking about when a particular figure of speech is used in discourse? All kinds of images may be mapped from a source to target domain, but the central meaning of the figurative expression may be missing if there is no point of reference. A general, but isolated, meaning may be construed if the actual sense of the word or figurative phase is defined according to a dictionary entry. This form of interpretation belongs to the type of semantics, according to which words are defined without context. In the following discussion, the debate about reference will raise the more specific notion of what will be termed here *referential semantics*.

With regard to the interpretation of meaning, a word may be construed according to a dictionary-type definition or a wider understanding according to the context. In the case of figurative language, it has been suggested that a poetic innovation in the form of a nominalistic metaphor essentially requires access to a wider context in order to understand the sense of the term.[1] Nominalism in philosophy proposes that "the mind can frame no single concept or image corresponding to any universal or general term"[2]. In other words, nominalistic metaphors are widely open to interpretation.

In addition, "wide interpretation" implies the relationship between the standard meaning of a term, i.e. the *signifié* in Saussurean terminology,[3] and the analogy between the usual referential point of the term and the actual reference in a text. This form of interpretation may be designated as referential semantics, whereby a sign X represents an object or concept X.[4] The problem arises that many words are highly

DOI: 10.4324/9781032130378-6

polysemous. The result is that a large number of concepts may be needed to pinpoint reference. Furthermore, a figure of speech such as a metaphor may not be restricted to one lexeme. It could also involve verbal expressions, which contain a series of metaphors.

Finally, there has been a long debate about whether such definitions necessarily require extra-linguistic reference.[5] Many interpretations could be given within the scope of polysemy, but they may not provide the full answer. For this reason, a fundamental argument here is that extra-linguistic information is very often required for interpretation in discourse.

6.2 *Mental Spaces*

Before looking at the extra-linguistic dimension, it would be useful to look at one particular approach to figurative meaning in CMT in the form of *mental spaces*.[6] Apart from meaning, the discussion of mental spaces is also a helpful one with regard to the mapping of reality which will be raised in the following chapters. As far as these two particular aspects are concerned, the main features of the theory have been outlined in the following way.[7]

Mental space theory offers a means of understanding reference, as well as the comprehension of stories, whether they are real or imagined. Four main types of spaces can be categorised as follows: time spaces (displacement into the past or future); space spaces (geographical displacement); domain spaces (the types of activities used) and hypothetical spaces (conditional situations, hypothetical possibilities and speculation).

In addition, it is suggested that spaces help understand reality. In other words, a reality space may be constructed around the mental representations of what we perceive. Knowledge creates a projected space and the same process applies to fictional spaces in which an ongoing narrative is built up. An example would be the sentence, "perhaps there is intelligent life on other worlds", which involves both a hypothetical and spatial projection from the environment on Earth.

Finally, two spaces may become intermingled into what is termed *conceptual blending*. This implies, for example, that two characters from different historical periods may be situated in the same scene. Again, blending can involve different categories such as cross-space mapping (the partial mapping of counterparts in two spaces); generic space (the abstraction of specific elements common to both spaces); and the blending of other associated spaces. With regard to literary discourse, the foregoing theory of mental spaces may be applied to theories on possible and discourse worlds.[8] These may be outlined in the following discussion.

6.3 Possible Worlds and Discourse Worlds

Within the realm of truth values, a possible world can only exist when two mental spaces, for example, are juxtaposed with statements that are not contradictory. The following two sentences cannot be combined in the same mental space: "alien intelligence exists" and "alien intelligence does not exist". This form of universal value is different if an event in our actual world is changed in the context of fiction. The sentence, "The Allies defeated the Axis in the Second World War", represents our actual world. If the Allies and Axis were changed around in the sentence, it would become a mental space reflecting a possible world, even if it alters the truth value in our actual world.

This process of formal logic established in a possible world can be adapted to *discourse worlds* in literature in order for a reader to understand narratives. Discourse worlds are thereby imaginary worlds conjured up by the reading of a text in order to understand events taking place in such settings. Mental spaces in the form of embedded worlds involving flashbacks, flashforwards, unrealised possibilities and so on, lead the reader through the fictional world. Protagonists can have virtual discourse worlds in their heads, which may represent fictional belief systems. A number of different categories within discourse worlds have also been established in these theories. With regard to truth values and meaning, the following could be selected: epistemic worlds (what characters believe to be true in their world); wish worlds (what characters wish might be different about their world) and fantasy worlds (the mental spaces of characters' dreams and wishes about their world).

An example of such sub-worlds can be seen in the first four lines of the following poem by John Keats[9]:

> When I Have Fears
>
> When I have fears that I may cease to be
> Before my pen has glean'd my teeming brain,
> Before high-piled books, in charact'ry,
> Hold like rich garners the full-ripen'd grain;
> > John Keats

A way of determining meaning and reference according to this approach is to examine the mental space in which the poem is situated.

It is about a poet who writes a great deal, illustrated by the sentence "hold like rich garners the full-ripen'd grain". This could be interpreted as a WRITING IS HARVESTING conceptual metaphor with the source domain depicted by high-piled books. The extensive literary productivity is symbolised by the rich garners in the target domain. The actual meaning of the metaphorical mental space is therefore clear but, in order to have a fuller contextual understanding, the reference point of the person involved is a requirement. In this sub-world, which could be a hypothetical world or wish world which involves fears of "ceasing to be" (dying), the pronoun "I" clearly denotes the person. However, does this refer to the poet, John Keats? In order to establish these facts, substantial information is required about the poet's life.

These theories have been formulated in relation to the reader's own interpretation. The present study, in order to establish ultimate origins, is concerned primarily with what is in the author's mind. Conceptual mapping processes in writing involve, to a large extent, the models of mental spaces and discourse worlds. They all have a link to reality or non-reality in the author's mind and certain aspects of this theory will be taken up in the debates to follow. However, investigation into the author's mind undoubtedly requires extra-linguistic information which is quite distinct from textual analysis. This also includes the notion of flexible truth values in the real world.

6.4 Reference in Conceptual Mappings

The discussion given above represents a broad overview of mental space theory, which can often determine the kinds of ideas figurative language might be referring to in textual analysis. The problems of reference in the real world, which is constantly changing, can first be demonstrated by a simple mathematical equation.

It will be suggested here that three points are integrated into a referential figurative mapping, which may be compared to the form of a triangle. The basic projection of a mapping involves the transfer of a concept at point A in the source domain to point B in the target domain. This forms one side of the triangle. The other sides are linked to point C, which is represented by the reference, otherwise known as the referent or referential point. The A–B side is necessarily linked to C if both textual and extra-linguistic information is required to understand why the figurative mapping is being used. In addition, the nature of the reference can have an impact on the types of images being transferred from A to B.

The following example will demonstrate this model, which can also involve fixed idiomatic expressions whose intrinsic meaning is well known. With a simple example taken from the press, the expression "a red line" will be examined to outline the problems of missing or unclear reference. It also implies the reference of personal pronouns, "I" and "we". The intrinsic semantics of these pronouns are clear, but additional information is required to define who is actually involved.

The following type of ongoing discourse is a common feature in the press and can apply to many forms of press releases. In 2012, during the early stages of the Syrian conflict, which continues at the time of writing, the President of the United States, Barack Obama, used the red line metaphor when referring to the use of chemical weapons by the Syrian President, Bachar el-Assad. Obama stated at a press conference:

> We have been very clear to the Assad regime, but also to other players on the ground, that a red line for us is if we start seeing a whole bunch of chemical weapons moving around or being utilized.[10]

The metaphor mapping involves a source domain relating to the notion of the "movement of chemical weapons" (point A) and the target domain to the fixed expression "a red line" (point B). In other words, the former concept is seen in terms of the latter, the red line imposing a limit on the movement of chemical weapons. The nature of multiple flexibility in this example can be seen as the political situation evolved. Due to geopolitical events at the time, the continual press releases associated with Obama's initial statement led to referents being modified with regard to pronouns in the statement. The pronoun "we", for example, was later changed to "the whole world" (at point C):

> First of all, I didn't set a red line; the whole world set a red line.[11]

The question then becomes: who is setting the red line? Furthermore, who is "we" and who is "the whole world"? In this case, not only the geopolitical context would be required to understand the changes in reference but also uses of rhetorical expressions such as "the whole world". Extra-linguistic information is essential here to establish the overall meaning of the idiomatic phrase and why the person is using it. In linguistic terms, some scholars have even suggested that the referent becomes more important than trying to define the semantic aspects of the metaphor, claiming the focus has to be changed from senses to referents if a degree of realism is required.[12] As suggested above, the impact of the reference on the model can lead to changes in the A–B mapping, which involves innovations in the fixed expression. If a press commentator agreed with Obama's rhetoric, for example, the image was a thick red line. If not, the colour moved from red to pink, if the rhetoric was felt to be not strong enough:

Obama's **thick red line** on Syria[13]

"The line moved **from red to pink**", White said. "When you start waffling and wobbling on what the 'red line' means and what you will do to enforce it, that will show weakness".[14]

6.5 Philosophy and Reference

The point to be emphasised here is that reference, as well as truth values, are forever changing according to ongoing advances in our knowledge about facts, events and situations. This fundamental argument will be used in the following chapters on the link between conceptual mapping and the distinction used here between real and fantasy worlds. The real world, based on personalised truth values at a given point in time, may be also used in the context of fiction.

The actual notion of reference has been a fascinating subject of discussion in many related disciplines. Debates on reference, not only in political discourse but also in literature and philosophy, have thus involved changing theories according to our knowledge of the world at any given point in time. One major figure in this area was the German philosopher, Gottlob Frege[15]. He put forward the example in philosophy of the planet Venus being construed as two different gods by the Ancient Greeks: Phosphorous (the morning star) and Hesperus (the evening star). Due to the planet's appearance at different times of the day, the Ancient Greeks assumed two planets were involved. As a result of our knowledge of astronomy today, the referent has changed and it is clear that the construal of meaning must therefore be based on the perceiver's viewpoint at any given time. This aspect, to be discussed in chapter 9, appears to be normally based on what is termed in cognitive studies as deixis and ego-centred perception. However, it also depends on the limitations of worldly knowledge and changing circumstances. Consequently, it likewise leaves the vast subject of truth values in meaning and reference open to debate. In philosophy, the controversial topic of truth values has been argued from many different angles throughout the 20th century.[16]

6.6 Hidden Reference Theory

This study suggests that, in order to pinpoint the origins leading to the use of figurative language, an analysis of reference is essential. It will be argued here that reference can be assessed at two conceptual levels: the first concerns the actual mapping of figures of speech in a given text (Level 1) and the second, at a much deeper level, is associated with ideas and influences concealed, to a greater or lesser extent, in the mind of the speaker or writer (Level 2). This will be termed *hidden reference theory* since referential points may not at first be obvious in a written text and research into the personal experience of a writer is required.

Studies on metaphor and reference, as in the case of mental spaces, generally deal with the first level of textual mappings and discourse analysis. In other words, the referent is normally denoted as a concept established in either the source or target domains of the mapping itself and within a given corpus. Level 2 reference, which will be outlined in more detail below, is a much wider notion of reference concerning the personal origins of figurative language and thought in the language user and innovator.

6.7 Textual Reference

In addition to mental spaces, some theoretical discussion of Level 1 reference is necessary here, particularly with regard to the cognitive framework outlined above. In accordance with textual mapping, several analyses dealing with specific features of figurative language illustrate the kinds of definitions of referents proposed so far. One particular theory concerns the distinction between metaphor and metonymy. It is claimed, for example, that interpreting a metonymic expression involves retrieving and retaining source as well as target referents in a mapping, whereas metaphor requires the interpreter to extract at least one property of the source referent and transfer it to the target.[17]

According to this hypothesis, the types of referents alluded to are naturally concepts in the source or target domain of a textual mapping. Further views on the distinction between metaphor and metonymy also highlight the fundamental role of reference in the latter. It has been stated that:

> metaphor and metonymy are different kinds of processes. Metaphor is principally a way of conceiving one thing in terms of another, and its primary function is understanding. Metonymy,

on the other hand, has primarily a referential function, that is, it allows us to use one entity to stand for another.[18]

Another distinction, in which referents in source and target domains are implied, concerns the labels of "literal" or "metaphorical". In the expression "many corporate lawyers are well-paid sharks", the sharks image has been termed a metaphorical referent since fish cannot literally be paid. In contrast, the concept "glacier" in the expression, "science is a glacier", is a literal-referent metaphor since the term literally exists.[19] The importance of this distinction in reference is no doubt due to the fact that the latter metaphor is perhaps more difficult to interpret than sharks and would require more contextual information. However, it may be assumed to have attributes such as the notions of "cold", "dispassionate" or "slow" and these images could be transferred to the concept of science. In short, the literal referent is understood literally and the metaphorical referent is understood metaphorically,[20] requiring different conceptual processes in the transfer between domains. These definitions again concern referents in the source and target domains of a textual mapping.

Further distinctions in the properties of this kind of referent, likewise with regard to literal and metaphorical reference in mappings, have led to the notion of single and dual reference in structures such as epithets. This may suggest that certain types of metaphorical pattern, as in the case of epithets, can actually determine the number of referents.[21] These different notions of reference therefore concern various types of metaphor. However, all cases involve fixed textual mapping.

A move towards the inclusion of reference within a wider context can be seen in hypotheses such as deliberative metaphor theory (DMT). Here, the role of referents is allocated to the parameter of a situation model as part of other features regarding utterances that are multi-functional. Among these are also the surface text, a text base and a context model.[22] There appears to be a distinction here between concepts in text bases and their referents.[23] In cognitive psychology, a situation model refers indeed to a mental representation which extracts information out of textually and verbally described situations.[24] In other words, a text often requires delving into information around the context. From a position of simply stating the types of reference in a given mapping, questions start being raised as to why such referents are used.

Reference and the importance of context is a fundamental issue, which has been raised more recently in metaphor studies, reinforcing the dynamic aspect discussed above. It is claimed that:

context is never predetermined and objectively existing; it must be created (and recreated) in the course of the communicative process (…) Meaning construction is a dynamic and creative process that results from the interaction of (more or less) conventional meanings (…) based on embodied experience, on the one hand, and the contextual factors deemed to be relevant, on the other.[25]

The Level 1 reference theories discussed so far thus deal with links to referents in textual mapping. They include distinctions such as literal and figurative meaning, as well as categorisations in figurative language like metaphor and metonymy or epithets. More importantly with regard to the present study, a reference often requires additional information around the context and the latter is in constant change. More or less conventional meanings can lead into dynamic and creative processes. With the very basic example of the red line metaphor above, it can be seen that a conventional expression may develop any number of references, which require further contextual information for precise interpretation.

The theories mentioned above involve creativity and interpretation in discourse which, in the literary field, concern narrative. Depending on the type of narrative, whether it is straightforward or more complex, the nature of a reference in figurative thought may become essential in the interpretation of the plot. Furthermore, the types of linguistic and conceptual innovation involved in narrative may vary between relatively conventional to non-conventional social, historical or psychological settings.

To summarise the discussions so far, it has been suggested that creativity in figurative language starts with the structural patterns of language which also vary according to individual languages. Behind language structure are thought processes. Within a cognitive framework, these processes depend on factors such as physiological and environmental conceptualisation. Cultural history influences the creation of figurative language according to factors like the networking of conceptual metaphors and their traditional social or economic values. Reference is required in discourse to establish the meaning of figurative mappings and to determine the reasons behind ongoing changes in the images used.

Language, thought, cultural history and reference are therefore the first four stages in setting up analytical levels in the search for origins. Turning more precisely to the field of literature, the fifth stage of the six-tier model delves into narrative. This aspect provides the essential component of contextual information. The next chapter will examine this feature in relation to comparative literature with a multicultural and multilingual background.

Notes

1. Monte (2020).
2. Merriam-Webster: https://www.merriam-webster.com/dictionary/nominalism [Accessed: 12/06/2020].
3. De Saussure (1916).
4. Kleiber (1984: 79).
5. Kleiber (1997).
6. Fauconnier (1994, 1997).
7. See Stockwell (2002: 96ff) for a fuller discussion of this theory.
8. idem (2002: 92ff).
9. idem (2002: 146ff).
10. http://www.whitehouse.gov/the-press-office/2012/08/20/remarks-president-white-house-press-corps [Accessed: 12/04/2021].
11. http://www.whitehouse.gov/the-press-office/2013/09/04/remarks-president-obama-and-prime-minister-reinfeldt-sweden-joint-press- [Accessed: 12/04/2021].
12. Hausman (1983: 181).
13. http://www.bbc.com/news/world-us-canada-23800031 [Accessed: 12/04/2021].
14. http://www.cbsnews.com/news/assessing-red-lines-as-obama-mulls-syria-attack/ [Accessed: 12/04/2021].
15. Frege (1892).
16. Kripke (1980); Putnam (1981).
17. Warren (2002: 113).
18. Lakoff and Johnson (1980: 36).
19. Bowdle and Gentner (2005).
20. Kittay (1987: 302).
21. Bezuidenhout (2008).
22. McNamara and Magliano (2009).
23. Steen (2017: 8).
24. Zwaan and Radvansky (1998).
25. Kövecses (2015: 71ff).

7 Textual Reference in the Form of Narrative

7.1 Variants of Love

Our search for the origins of figurative language will continue here with the relationship between love and the symbol of death, discussed in chapter 4, according to specific narratives found in European literature. Before doing so, an attempt to define love would be useful, as it can naturally represent a wide variety of different concepts. One dictionary definition encompassing such a wide range of conceptualisation is as follows: "a feeling or disposition of deep affection or fondness for someone, typically arising from a recognition of attractive qualities, from natural affinity, or from sympathy and manifesting itself in concern for the other's welfare and pleasure (...); great liking, strong emotional attachment; (similarly) a feeling or disposition of benevolent attachment experienced towards a group or category of people, and (by extension) towards one's country or another impersonal object of "affection".[1]

This definition covers a large range of feelings in the emotion of love, but perhaps not all. Another more precise type of delineation is the suggestion that love can be divided into five main categories according to Ancient Greek terminology.[2] There is only one word in English, which requires other additions such as compounding, for more refined definitions. However, the traditional Greek terms use different words for each category: "family love" (*storge*), "friendship" (*philia*), "physical love" (*eros*), "religious love" (*agape*) and "love of things" (*khreia*). Again, this kind of categorisation may be problematic since they can overlap or there is not a term for such concepts as "marital love".[3] Another complication in the terms used in Ancient Greece is that the list has been the subject to various types of semantic

DOI: 10.4324/9781032130378-7

change in specific items. For example, it has been claimed that the Ancient Greek term *eros* actually referred to all aspects of a relationship between two people in love, whereas it has changed semantically towards physical love in modern European languages.[4] It will be seen that an exception occurs when the unique term *eros* is used in literary or philosophical discussions on the subject of love, in contrast to morphological derivations of the base lexeme, as in "erotic", "eroticism", etc.

The first part of this study will focus on the notion of romantic love between two people, and thus it entails the original concept of Greek *eros*. It normally excludes categories such as *khreia*, but it will be seen that romantic love, particularly in literary discourse and in specific historical periods, often overlaps with additional categories in this classification, such as *agape*.

7.2 Social Attitudes in D. H. Lawrence

Returning to Lawrence's postulated conceptual metaphor of LOVE IS DEATH in his novel, *The Rainbow*, the narrative contains many references to the love/death relationship between Ursula and Skrebensky mentioned in the first chapter. In many ways, it represents an impossible form of romantic love, even though both strive to make it successful. As far as the plot is concerned, an overall picture of Ursula's situation may be depicted in the following way.

She is the granddaughter of Tom Brangwen who married a Polish refugee, Lydia. The first part of the novel deals with the difficult relationships within the Brangwen family and, in particular, the struggles between her parents, Will and Anna. Ursula attempts to find fulfilment in love within the confines of a conformist society. She has a same-sex relationship with a teacher before the doomed affair with Skrebensky. However, the novel ends on a positive note with Ursula foreseeing a new beginning for humanity in the symbol of a rainbow, and hence the title of the book.

With regard to the love/death figurative language in the narrative, it was seen above that the amorous encounter between Ursula and Skrebensky in the moonlight leads to a number of ongoing linguistic metaphors in discourse. A variety of secondary mappings can be extrapolated from the base LOVE IS DEATH metaphor portrayed in different scenarios. Following the lines of a cognitive linguistic analysis, one is the idea of "coming back to life again" through the force of love. This could be postulated in an extended LOVE IS BACK FROM THE DEAD mapping:

And she began **to caress him to life again. For he was dead**. And she intended that he should never know, never become aware of what had been. She would bring him **back from the dead** without leaving him one trace of fact to remember his annihilation by.

Another more concrete concept is poison, associated with death and the notions of "burning" and "corroding", such as the "salt-burning" metaphor found in other passages in the novel. This could be represented by a LOVE IS POISON mapping. In the same paragraph, the physical act of kissing evokes the notion death in a LOVE IS A DEATH-LIKE MOUTH image:

> He strove subtly, but with all his energy, to enclose her, to have her. And always she was burning and brilliant and hard as salt, and deadly. Yet obstinately, all his flesh burning and corroding, as if he were invaded by some consuming, **scathing poison**, still he persisted, thinking at last he might overcome her. Even, in his frenzy, he sought for her mouth with his mouth, though it was like **putting his face into some awful death.**

In all cases, Skrebensky is metaphorically dying in the love relationship. One of the main reasons behind it appears to be the fact that, according to traditional literary critics, he represents a rather shallow personality unable to have a proper relationship with a woman. In addition, the stronger, female personality of Ursula tends to overcome him, leading to his annihilation[5]. In addition, Skrebensky is depicted as a somewhat 'mechanical' character with traditional, conservative views in contrast to Ursula who wished to be liberated from the social customs of the time. In this way, he epitomises the conformist society around her. It was essentially these views in the powerful scenes, such as the meeting among the haystacks described above, which led to its censorship in 1915. By representing the social customs of the period, Skrebensky attempted to convince Ursula that she needed to play the traditional role of an army officer's wife. It was an impossible task for her, and it could therefore be deduced that such points of conflict represent the referential points of the love/death figurative mappings repeated throughout the narrative. Furthermore, the moonlight scenes added symbolic overtones whose deeper reference will be discussed in more detail below.

Other examples of love and death conceptual metaphors in comparative literature can be seen with very different referential points. The following debate is not so much concerned by the innovative types of linguistic metaphors and cognitive images, which are possible in literary discourse, and which can be seen in a very extensive way in Lawrence's writing, as the much more complex forms of reference which lead to narrative origins of figurative language. An interesting case is Simone De Beauvoir.

7.3 Existentialism in Simone De Beauvoir

The figurative language of love and death has very different origins in the narrative structures of novels such as Beauvoir's *L'Invitée (She Came to Stay)*.[6] The narrative sources in this novel move onto the realm of philosophy but also include revolutionary ideals on social customs with regard to traditional love relationships.[7] Due to the relative complexity of the plot, only the main details will be described here.

The three main protagonists are Pierre (a theatre manager), Françoise (who works together with Pierre and is his lover) and Xavière (a young girl who wishes to start a new life away from home and is invited by the former two to join them in Paris). Pierre feels romantically attracted to Xavière, which leads to Françoise feeling jealous, but she nevertheless wants to maintain a strong feeling of friendship towards Xavière. Pierre also feels ambiguous about the situation since he values his relationship with Françoise but, at times, feels strongly attracted to Xavière.

Despite the deepening relationship between Pierre and Xavière, Françoise wishes to keep the two relationships and a love triangle develops. At the beginning, she feels this would be the ideal solution and believes a harmonious, polyamorous situation would also be a valuable aim in life to strive for. However, other secondary characters become involved in the triangle and, as the narrative progresses, it becomes clear that Françoise finds it increasingly difficult to endure the feelings of jealousy engendered primarily by Xavière. Despite further efforts to harmonise the situation with her, Françoise finally decides that Xavière's presence has become too much for her and she kills her rival by turning on the gas in Xavière's apartment.

The good intentions of Françoise ("a well-bonded couple alone is a fine thing but how much richer it can be if three people love each other very deeply"), are clear at the beginning of the novel, but later turn to metaphors of death-related images. In this novel, she feels that the evolving love relationships are becoming unbearable. Her first serious talks with Pierre are filled with criticism about his "dead" feelings of love which resemble sepulchres and mummies:

You always want your feelings to be the same, you need them close to you, well organised, unchanging, and even if nothing is left inside, you couldn't care less. They are like the Gospel's **bleached sepulchres**; they shine on the outside, they are solid, faithful, now and again you can even polish them up again with beautiful words (...). But they should never be opened, you'll only find **ashes** and **dust**. (...) It's a serious matter, I'm sure I'm telling the truth; your feelings are unshakeable, they can survive for centuries because they are **mummies**.

She Came to Stay, Simone De Beauvoir

When the narrative finally turns Francoise's strong feelings towards Xavière, the metaphors become stark and varied. She feels her role in the love triangle has an insiduous and evil influence on the relationship between Françoise and Pierre. The symbols used are "funeral shades" in reference to the lighting in Xavière's room and the "gloominess and evil" in her look:

Over there, in the **funeral shades** of her room, Xavière was sitting, wrapped in her brown dressing-gown, looking gloomy and evil; Pierre's sorrowful love humbly stroking her feet. Françoise wandered around in the streets, rejected and putting up with the old remains of her worn-out affection.

The feeling of death towards the end of the story builds up with symbols of "poisoned atmosphere" and "sticky smell":

She took off her coat. She had to speak. But how? She could not mention Gerbert's secrets, and yet she could not live in **this poisoned atmosphere**. Between the smooth, blue panes and in the **sticky smell** of sun-tan lotion, Pierre's aggrieved feelings and Françoise's the low jealousy undoubtedly existed. They had to be destroyed. Only Xavière could destroy them.

This atmosphere builds up to a climax during which Françoise decides to kill Xavière.

Physiological metaphors of burning and black lava running through her veins and heart push her towards this final desperate act when she has finally made a choice in the relationship by choosing herself. In other words, she had decided what she needed to do for herself in order to get out of the situation:

Black and torrid lava flowed through her veins (…) the **burning lava flowed and consumed her heart** (…) she had at last made a choice. She had chosen herself.

The unconventional scenario of the novel is, to a large extent, based on the philosophy of existentialism. This philosophical reference in the novel is the variant developed by Sartre, whose origins go back to Kierkegaard, in which everyone is responsible for his or her own acts.[8] In short, a human being is born without pre-defined values and aims but is defined by the acts performed throughout his or her life. The sum of these acts at death determine the "essence" of each person. Each person is alone in these decisions. For this reason, the novel finishes with the narrator's statement that Françoise had at last made a choice on her own account. The result is one of impossible love and a LOVE IS DEATH scenario. These represent very briefly the main arguments for the figurative language in the network of relationships in the narrative, although there are deeper issues behind which will be taken up below. Among these are the quest for identity and the confrontation with other people in life.

Before doing so, a final author writing within the love/death equation will be analysed here: Hermann Hesse and his novel, *Steppenwolf*. As in Beauvoir's work, the ideas behind his novel go very deep, but in a different way.

7.4 Personal Psychology in Hermann Hesse

The following passage taken from *Steppenwolf* sums up, to a large extent, the attitudes towards love felt by the main protagonist of the story, Hermann Haller:

In this beautiful, calm night, many images of my life went through my mind, which I normally had experienced as being empty, impoverished and without images. Now, being in **the magic shroud of Eros**, the source of all these pictures ran deep and intensely through me. For some moments, my heart stood still from the delight and sadness evoked by the rich picture gallery of my life and how full of distant **eternal stars and constellations** the poor steppenwolf's soul had been. In the infinite blueness, childhood and Mother appeared to glimpse tenderly and blissfully over a distant and faded stretch of mountains. The choir of my circle of friends rang out, beginning with the incredible Hermann, Hermine's soul brother. Fragrant and unearthly, **like moist, blooming water flowers,** the images of many women I had loved, admired and praised were swimming before me, few of whom I had had within my reach or tried to possess.

And yet that was only the outer surface: within, everything was full of significance, tension and destiny. While I was lovingly and tenderly occupied with the small, sweet and moving sides to love, and seemed to be swimming in the warm waters of happiness, I felt deep down that my fate was striving forward head over heels, beating and kicking like a timid steed, towards **an abyss, a plunge into the depths,** full of fear, longing and sacrificing my life.
Steppenwolf, Hermann Hesse

In the first paragraph, it can be seen that images of love for his childhood days and his mother are represented by an upwards orientation to the conventional images of eternal stars and constellations in the night sky. Despite the sadness felt by the distance of such images, there is delight in their rich picture gallery and in the tender and blissful glimpse of mountains which also evoke memories of his life. The generally upwards orientation signifies positive attitudes toward loving memories. In addition, romantic love is depicted by other typical concepts such as blooming water flowers.

However, the second paragraph is in sharp contrast. The downward movement of a plunge into the depths of an abyss symbolises the fear of romantic love in the novel. The passage therefore represents a very good example of the cognitive *Spatialisation of Form Hypothesis* outlined in chapter 4, according to which upward orientation is generally positive and vice versa for downward orientation. Where does this contrast come from in the narrative and where are the references? There are a certain number of parallel features with *The Rainbow*, such as the conflict between conformist and non-conformist society but, in general, the plot is more complex and focuses on intricate psychological characteristics. The images appear to be relatively straightforward, but the reasons behind them go very deep. The reference points in the orientational images given above are closely linked to the psychological state of the protagonist, Hermann Haller.

The following main points related to Haller's psychology may be extracted from the plot as follows. The first is the fact that he believes there are two worlds within him: a high, spiritual world reflected by images in the novel relating to an interest in traditional ways of life such as, for example, the church and classical music. The other is represented by a low, animalistic one related to other settings and circumstances such as the "frivolous" dance-halls of the time. The "wild" nature of the latter represents the title of the book: "the wolf of the steppes". The second point is that Haller has suicidal tendencies, which oscillate between feeling that he may take his life one day but that it could lead to the grandiose feeling of being "immortal". These aspects are entangled with his difficulty of letting himself go in order to be able to love someone and hence the feelings described in the passage above.

The intricacies of the overall plot reveal in a complex manner how these feelings come to the fore. While wandering aimlessly around a city one day, Haller meets someone carrying an advertisement for a magic theatre and who gives him a book entitled *Treatise on the Steppenwolf*. To his astonishment, the book actually describes Haller himself in an uncanny way. He later meets the man who gave him the book, and he suggests Haller should go to a local dance-hall rather than to the magic theatre. He eventually goes to the dance-hall against his will and meets a woman called Hermine. She introduces him to his future lover, Maria, who frequently goes to the dance-hall and who is linked to the "fun-loving life" of dancing and, in addition, to casual drug-taking. The final part of the novel deals with Haller's actual visit to the metaphorical magic theatre where he enters the psychological world of fantasy. The horseshoe-shaped "theatre" has a corridor with a mirror on one side and a large number of doors on the other. Haller opens five labelled doors, each of which symbolise different periods of his life. This experience actually represents the point at which Haller comes to terms with his inner psychology and constitutes a "trip through hell" in order to find the answers. It matches the bipolar feature of his attitude towards love. Further insight into the psychological implications of this state of mind will be discussed in the next chapter.

The figurative images that Hesse uses in the passage above first reflect the love for Haller's childhood memories and for the women he has encountered in his life. At the present moment, he is directly involved in the realm of *Eros*, according to the Ancient Greek term of romantic love and adopted by Freudian psychology. However, he is also confronted with feelings of death. Haller's meeting with Maria becomes complicated since his resistance to a fun-loving life prevents him from developing a natural relationship with the woman in this type of world. The magic shroud of Eros in the relationship therefore signifies, on the one hand, a beautiful environment along the lines of the meaning "magical" and a desire to enjoy life, but on the other, a 'shroud', since he is lost in a relationship filled with conflicting emotions. At one point, he feels pleasure and, at another, fear and sacrifice. Again, these bi-polar emotions are explained in terms of Freudian psychology in the novel.

Within the orientational schemas of cognitive linguistics outlined above, the basic LOVE IS DEATH conceptual metaphor in the context thereby has secondary conceptual mappings in the form of LOVE IS AN ABYSS or LOVE IS A PLUNGE INTO THE DEPTHS metaphors. As a result, the point of reference in the mapping triangle of the scenario is Haller's complicated relationship with Maria. The ambivalent nature between a "magic shroud" and an "abyss" signifies that, in the former, he is letting himself go and enjoying life, and in the latter, he is trying to pull himself up again to a higher, spiritual level. Consequently, he feels that Maria's "frivolous" environment is not one which is suitable for him and he has the premonition that the love relationship is ultimately doomed. The author chooses conventional images of an abyss and depths to convey the feeling of doom in this complex mixture of emotions.

The psychological aspect of the scenario is very much a Freudian one based on the two main categories of *Eros* and *Thanatos*. They may be applied to the changing moods of the protagonist, Haller, in his encounters with Maria. Freud suggests that life instincts are responsible for the former and are based on survival, pleasure and reproduction.[9] The Ancient Greek god of love, *Eros,* symbolises this life drive. On the other hand, there also appears to be an unconscious wish to die which is brought out by the fact that people who have witnessed traumatic events, such as war, are often drawn towards them again in their dreams. This compulsion is a death drive symbolised by the Ancient Greek god of death, *Thanatos*.[10] The death drive is in contradiction to the desire to survive, have pleasure and reproduce. This psychological model reflects the scenario very closely.

A comparison of Hesse's figurative language with Lawrence's works reveals a parallel with a LOVE IS DEATH conceptual metaphor arising, to some extent, from a desire to break away from existing social norms at the time. However, the origins, based on narrative structures, diverge at this point. The heroine of *The Rainbow*, Ursula Brangwen, attempts to break away from the social customs of her family environment, resulting in an analogy of love with death on the part of Skrebensky. The origins of the love/death scenario in *Steppenwolf* are based to a much larger degree on the aspect of individual psychology. The life and death drives in Haller appear to determine the love/death equation. Despite the trials and tribulations of the love relationships in the novels, both plots end on a positive note: a new beginning for humanity in *The Rainbow* and a decrease in inner emotional torments induced by the fantasy world depicted at the end of *Steppenwolf*.

At this point, it can be summarised that the narratives of the three different novels discussed above have a common thread in the form of a LOVE IS DEATH scenario in which the notion of impossible love is implied in each narrative. The contextual reasons for this common conceptual metaphor are extremely varied. Broadly speaking, the roots of the problem in *The Rainbow* arise in the nature of social customs at the time and its impact on the constrained life that Ursula has in her love relationships. In the second novel, *She Came to Stay*, the principles of thinking and actions by Françoise in relationship to the other participants in the love triangle are determined by an existentialist way of thinking and therefore from a philosophical point of view predominant at the time. In the third novel, *Steppenwolf,* the narrative roots of the love/death scenario can be found in the psychological bipolarity of the main protagonist, Haller.

This discussion represents what could therefore be called Level 1 regarding textual reference in the production of figurative language. Level 2 represents biographical or semi-biographical information about the author. This suggests that the original thoughts behind the type of language created are based on personal experience in life. As has been suggested, a biographical feature does not necessarily exist in all literary works, but it logically appears to be a very common one. The second part (Level 2) of textual reference, which has also been a controversial point of view in literary criticism, will be explored in the next chapter as part of the final stage of personal experience in the six-tier model.

Notes

1. Online Oxford Dictionary: https://www.thefreedictionary.com/Oxford+English+Dictionary+Online
2. Tissari (2003: 32–33).
3. idem. Tissari (2003: 33).
4. Wlosok (1975: 165–179).
5. Daiches (1960); Spilka (1963).
6. Beauvoir (1943).
7. For a fuller discussion on the notion of conceptual networking between underlying figurative constructs and linguistic metaphors in comparative literature, see Trim (2021a).
8. Sartre (1946).
9. Freud [1920] (1990).
10. Stekel (1911) originally introduced the term.

8 Personal Biography in Figurative Language

8.1 Narrative and Personal Biography

The final stage in the development of a six-tier model, which traces the components in figurative language back to its ultimate origins, thus involves the personal biographical interpretation of the authors themselves. The clues we have unearthed along this path of investigation thereby lead from the structure of specific languages themselves, through the realm of figurative thought, cultural history, the notion of reference, narrative discourse and, finally, to the aspect of personal biographies. These are mapped onto each other, and tie up together, in a final stage which may reveal why an author has put pen to paper in his or her particular style.

There are, no doubt, examples in which there is no direct connection at all. It may just concern an author's interest in a particular subject. However, there appear to be many examples which not only reveal a link to an author's personal experience but which are self-evident, or even described explicitly by the author. The interesting point here is to investigate the ways in which types of metaphors or symbolism used by a particular writer may have a direct link to his or her world. In other words, they may be presented in fiction but originate within the lives of the people who write them.

The network of conceptual mapping, however, can become relatively complex. Both the worlds of personal experience and fiction may interact between real and fantasy worlds in each dimension. Indeed, there are multiple mapping processes in literary discourse. A protagonist in a fictional dimension may conceptualise his or her environment as a real world within the plot, or it may actually represent a fantasy world within fiction. Furthermore, this aspect can be ambiguous within the

DOI: 10.4324/9781032130378-8

narrative. Finally, links to an author's personal biography may be traced back to either a real world or a fantasy world within an author's personal life. This complexity should become clearer with literary examples analysed in the discussions that follow. The result can represent a mosaic of conceptual mapping.

The complexity emerging from the analysis of personal experience varies according to the type of novel involved. Biographical information acts as an ultimate referential point of figurative language. It goes beyond a fictional character to the author's own life. Due to the varying types of proximity of a narrative to its authorship, this Level 2 reference can be a particularly invisible one. Facts may not be clearly stated in black and white and often depend on interpretation. They may appear to be relatively definitive. On the other hand, opinions about them often vary between the views of literary critics or readers' interpretations. In the case of an author claiming a link to personal biography, the narrative may also be "distorted" to some extent to fit in with an author's way of observing past life. Such is the case of the novel, *The Burning Girl,* by Claire Messud.[1]

8.2 *"Distortion" of Personal Lives*

The story here is about the relationship between two girls who have been close friends since nursery school. The narrative concerns the schooldays of Julia and Cassie and how their paths diverge in adolescence. Julia actually represents the author, Claire Messud who, in an interview, claimed that the depiction of the protagonist is not actually "my life" or my "personality", but rather "my story as I tell it to myself".[2] In other words, she writes according to an observation of her own life and the narrative she develops in the novel. Biographical reality can become transformed to some extent as a result of the developing narrative which "models identities and forms distorting mirrors" which the writer observes in retrospect.

The profound diversity in the origins of figurative words can be seen in the word "burning", as in the title, which is semantically very different from the "salt-burning" metaphor in D. H. Lawrence's novel, *The Rainbow.* Very often, not only an exploration is required with regard to an author's life but also, as explained in preceding chapters, to the historical route of the expression from which it was taken. It has been claimed that the epigraph of *The Burning Girl* is from Elizabeth Bishop's poem, *Casabianca:*

Love's the boy stood on the burning deck
trying to recite "the boy stood on
the burning deck". Love's the son
stood stammering elocution
while the poor ship went down.

In other words, the burning deck is a long and intense friendship between two pre-teenage girls which collapses beneath them.[3] The theme of love, from melodrama to allegory, has been introduced into this poem from the original and well-known *Casabianca* poem written by Felicia Dorothea Hermans in 1826:

The boy stood on the burning deck
Whence all but he had fled
The flame that lit the battle's wreck
Shone round him o'er the dead.

Historically, the poem is based on a real-life incident during the Battle of the Nile in 1798. The boy is a folk-figure with the name of Giocante Casabianca. The twelve year-old boy was serving under his father on the French flagship *L'Orient* when it was hit by Nelson's British fleet. Hermans wrote a poem about a son's devotion to his father. According to this information, it could therefore be assumed that Messud's use of the word 'burning' can be traced to this historical fact. In her novel, the end of a friendship is metaphorically mapped onto the concept of burning, as in the girl who "burns" and disappears in the friendship.

8.3 Criticism of Biographical Theories

Despite the evidence for close links between fiction and personal biography, it has been the subject of considerable controversy in the past within the field of literary criticism. One particular viewpoint will be briefly mentioned here. In the mid-20th century, the American New Criticism movement rejected the notion of autobiographical features in literary works.[4] Apart from the fact that an author may not wish his personal biography to be discussed in literary criticism, two main theories arose from the New Criticism movement: "The Intentional Fallacy" and the "Affective Fallacy". The first argues that it is not desirable to take into account the intentions of an author when assessing the merits of a literary piece of work. The second suggests that literary criticism based on the psychological influences of a novel represents an impressionistic and relativist assessment of the work. In other words, the author's biography should not be taken into consideration when analysing the language used.

It may be pointed out here that there seems to be a distinction between "intention" and "influence". An author may not necessarily intend to write down certain feelings in a conscious manner. Some expressions are often the result of an unconscious thought originating from his or her cultural or political environment. It may appear in a stylistic form if an author's intentions are not absolutely certain. A fundamental question is knowing whether feelings are premeditated before writing or whether they can be inferred from an analysis of the reference points in the text.[5]

8.4 Autobiography and Autofiction

One distinction in the debate has been the difference between *autobiography* and *autofiction*. The latter term[6] appears to be a step towards New Criticism but, at the same time, recognising the fact that fiction can be autobiographical. In other words, narrative may not have this intention, even though it is autobiographical. However, it would appear that very intentional processes can also come into play. Among the different stylistic types of autofiction are those in which the autobiographical references are deliberately changed in some form or other by the author. In this case, it may be assumed that the latter feels the need to portray his or her own life without aspects of self-identification becoming too apparent in the narrative. There are many examples such as Marcel Proust's novel, *In Search of Lost Time*.[7] Proust deliberately changed place names in the novel whose context appears, nevertheless, to be remarkably autobiographical.[8]

The intentions of the author may also be very specific as, for example, when the acceptability of ideas by the readership is in question. It may therefore create a distinction between the mind style of a fictional character, as discussed in chapter 4, and the style of the language used. It has also been suggested that the issue of the mind style of authors has been neglected for this reason.[9] As an example, the author, Flannery O'Connor, makes use of the grammatical structure 'as if' in her short stories so as not to directly portray her own convictions. In her essays, she confirms the fact that she views the world from the standpoint of Catholic orthodoxy but is aware she cannot force all her readership to accept this point of view. Hence the narratives follow the line of 'as if' comparisons.

Direct links between fictional characters and the actual mindsets of authors have been strengthened in more recent post-structuralist movements.[10] The argument here is that there are many types of *de facto* autobiographies such as essays, war memories, travel literature as well as pure autobiographies themselves. According to post-structuralism, these help in revealing factual information about real-life experience.

8.5 Individual Biographies

With this in mind, the three authors discussed in the previous chapter, Lawrence, Hesse and Beauvoir, will be taken up again from a biographical viewpoint. Research into this aspect can reveal the personal origins of the type of figurative concepts they use in their narratives. Compared to the application of particularly conventional types of figurative language they may use in their narratives, this level of reference can become more complex and delve deeply into the human psyche. The following discussion will be limited to the major features of influence on the figurative thought and language in the minds of the three authors.

8.6 Symbolic Influence in D. H. Lawrence

Various literary critics agree with the fact that a number of specific aspects in Lawrence's life influenced his writing and, in particular, the reference to death. It has been claimed that "recent research on D. H. Lawrence has emphasised the way that he used his own immediate life experience to shape and mould his writing".[11] In fact, Lawrence personally faced a number of events in his life which evoked the notion of death. The first is that he suffered from tuberculosis for a number of years before his death in 1930, although it appears he did not wish to include this aspect in his writing before the last 6 months of his life. Any reference to death in his late poetry appears to be a general attitude towards the subject rather than a reference to the prospects of his own death.[12]

The second point, which critics claim plays a major role, is the Freudian life/death instinct discussed in the previous chapter. The Eros/Thanatos dichotomy has been labelled with different terms. One is pleasure and death in which the pleasure principle is to serve death instincts. It has been suggested that he was a "virtual textbook embodiment of Freud's theories about the pleasure principle and the death instinct", whereby the aim of all life is death, a fact proven by the "terrible war which has just ended"[13] (World War I). There is no doubt that the war had a huge impact on Lawrence's way of thinking, in addition to the effects of industrialisation in the countryside after the Industrial Revolution. In his mind, it was as if humankind wished to destroy itself through the invention of war and industrial machines.

It has, in fact, been claimed that he saw the industrial complex of preparing for war as "Western society's suicide".[14] He felt that all implications in such wars suppressed the ideas of the individual and thereby impoverished human thinking. One interpretation of the protagonist Skrebensky, in his novel *The Rainbow*, symbolises the war since he is a soldier about to leave for the front, leaving Ursula behind. The actions of kissing and romantic love also reflected the horrors of the battlefield.

In a press article that Lawrence wrote in 1914, he describes the machine-like world of war at the front when he followed the army in Bavaria and observed the battle from a near-by hill:

> What work was there to do? Only mechanically to adjust the guns and fire the shot. What was there to feel? Only the unnatural suspense and suppression of serving a machine which, for ought we knew, was killing our fellow men, whilst we stood there, blind, without knowledge or participation, subordinate to the cold machine. This was the glamour and the glory of the war: blue sky overhead and living green country all around, but we, amid it all, a part in some iron insensate will, our flesh and blood, our soul and intelligence shed away, and all that remained of us a cold, metallic adherence to an iron machine.[15]

Another label for the pleasure/death distinction is "life and gravity", in which the latter signifies the acceptance of death. From a cognitive point of view, it can be seen that the pulling of gravity downwards leads to the conceptualisation of death in this particular orientational direction. From a Freudian approach, Lawrence completely agreed with Freud in the sense that explanations for the Great War could basically be found in the "psyche of modern Europeans which exposed a collective condition".[16]

A third point is the aspect of social class and family restrictions related to the protagonists' social attitude raised in the previous chapter. Related to this was also Lawrence's criticism of "Christianity's death obsession"[17] in society. However, a point to be emphasised here, with regard to the types of figurative language discussed in chapter 2, is the aspect of relationships. One, in particular, was Lawrence's personal relationship to his mother which undoubtedly played a major role in his life. This raises the question of the Freudian Oedipian complex. It appears that Lawrence was dominated by his mother, for whom he had a great affection, but which evolved into a love/hate relationship. The result was that it perhaps prevented him from developing a satisfactory relationship with the women he met in his life. Although he met his wife, Frieda, after some initial relationships, his first real love was with Jessie Chambers. This relationship was unsuccessful in the end, although the reasons for this are not entirely clear.

Indeed, a great deal has been written about male/female relationships in Lawrence's works. The frustrations he had with his mother may have arisen from the traditional domineering role of the woman in the household. It can be clearly seen in the novel, *Sons and Lovers*, in which Mrs. Morel has a dominant role over her husband when he is in the house. Several reasons have been put forward for the male/female roles in the family. One is the notion of Calvinist Protestantism in English society which determined the fact that conjugal relations stem mainly from patriarchal movements. Although the woman "lays down the law in the house", men have formulated the religious rules on this specific social structure.

Another comes from the more recent field of gender studies. In a sociological survey (2008) of "lad culture" in England, i.e. a "hedonistic and excessive party-going masculine culture, based on male camaraderie", it has been suggested that there are parallels between Lawrence's characters and the opinions stemming from this generalised social group. In other words, the vast majority of the group, taken from different social and cultural backgrounds, maintained that the woman in the house had the final word in their family environment. Fathers tended to be detached and/or subordinate. There is thus an ongoing culture of fixed male/female roles, which appears to be independent of religious movements.[18]

Be that as it may, the frustrations Lawrence had with his mother led him to a situation in which he wished to free himself from her. This is reflected in the moonlight scenes in his novels. The moon is traditionally a female symbol which can also evoke passion. An example of this can be seen in the scene of *Sons and Lovers* when Paul and Miriam are walking together one evening and they see a large orange moon staring at them. The result is that Paul is passionately aroused by the sight of the moon shining with this particular hue.

The moon also symbolises motherhood. In the same novel, Mrs. Morel takes refuge in the moonlight after a quarrel with her husband. In this scene, she is pregnant and the moonlight calms her nerves and her unborn child, Paul. The link to the mother in moonlight appears to be another problematic source in Lawrence's writing and hence his moonlight scenes are very austere. The passage at the beginning of chapter 2 symbolises the wish to break ties with a mother figure by destroying the reflection of the moon in the water. The amorous encounters of Ursula and Skrebensky among the haystacks described in *The Rainbow* also reflect the atmosphere of impossible love symbolised by the moonlit environment. Hence the use of innovations such as 'whitish-steely fires' or 'moon-conflagration'. Furthermore, their relationship in this austere environment led to an inversion of patriarchal/matriarchal values. Ursula wished to break free from the traditional patriarchal society embodied, in particular, by her father.

The result of Lawrence's way of thinking led to situations of impossible love in many of the relationships portrayed in his novels. Romantic love became a feature of mortality in an historical, cultural and social environment of humanity's madness. This attitude towards an association of love and death forms the origins of his personal points of reference and ways of thinking that surface in the language of his narratives. The same association can be found in the literary works of Simone De Beauvoir, but for quite different reasons, even though some parallel links may appear with regard to a rejection of social norms at the time.

8.7 The Philosophical Background to Simone De Beauvoir

Simone de Beauvoir witnessed social and historical events similar to D. H. Lawrence, although her life spanned a period which was a little later than his, 1908–1986, compared to Lawrence's shorter life from 1885 to 1930. As a result, war-time experiences and its environment were different since Beauvoir's life was concerned more with the Second World War rather than the first. This was particularly with regard to issues concerning Hitler's potential invasion in the 1930s and, finally, the German occupation of Paris. Despite this major impact on her early years, her writing reflected a major preoccupation with her rejection of specific social norms in France at the time.

Beauvoir was raised in the upper middle classes of Parisian society. A rift grew between her parents for financial reasons, among others and, due to a loss of income, the family was obliged to take up residence in an area in which her father felt he had lost social standing. According to Catholic principles, the mother had a major role in a daughter's upbringing and education. This also concerned the upbringing of boys. However, it was to a lesser extent when the boys became older.[19] In some ways, this would also correspond to the active role of the mother in Lawrence's upbringing within the home environment.

Furthermore, it has been suggested that the opening up of higher education studies to women, which Beauvoir took up in philosophy at the Sorbonne, was initially implemented by a patriarchal system. It has been suggested that the Republican elite, in power from 1870 onwards, aimed to educate wives within a certain political framework in order to avoid any confrontation with their Republican husbands.[20] In this way, there are certain parallels with an authoritative Calvinist Protestantism mentioned above in Lawrence's case. However, the suggestion of a social context such as "lad culture" is far removed. Beauvoir was to become an adamant feminist within the context of her relationship with the philosopher, Jean-Paul Sartre, whom she met at the Sorbonne.

Their lives entered a profound, non-conformist way of life, partly as a rejection to her bourgeois background, and partly on the basis of Sartre's philosophical convictions. Their belief in open, amorous relationships undoubtedly led to the scenario in Beauvoir's first novel, *She Came to Stay*. After a geographical separation in their teaching professions, Beauvoir and Sartre eventually found posts in Paris together. As a result of their contacts with students in different places, Beauvoir had a homosexual relationship with a young girl in Rouen in 1934, Olga Kosakievicz. At a later stage, Olga also became Sartre's mistress. In addition, Beauvoir had a relationship with one of Sartre's students, Jacques-Laurent Bost, who later married Olga. This intertwined network of relationships became known as "the family". Despite the turbulent state of affairs, Beauvoir maintained her relationship with Sartre until his death in 1980.

This "turbulent", real-life scenario was undoubtedly inspiration for the plot of *She Came to Stay*. It is claimed that Sartre's desire for Olga led to the breakdown of the initially good intentions of a harmonious trio in the novel.[21] The story, due to its framework of existentialist philosophy, encompassed the notion of "authentic" love which entailed the ideas of freedom, consciousness and the rejection of all feelings of possession. However, different emotional feelings are intermingled in the plot such as those associated with love, friendship, jealousy and experiencing new relational encounters in life.

A number of Freudian psychological threads have been interpreted in the novel such as Francoise's Oedipian tendencies.[22] Instead of exploring parent/child complexes, however, another path of clues concerning origins more relevant to love/death conceptualisation will be examined here. The following discussion will take up a philosophical theory traced back to Hegel. Indeed, it is clear that the existentialist focus in the story stems from his philosophy, according to which self-consciousness can only be determined through the eyes of other people. It thus implies identification with another consciousness so that a self-image may be obtained by looking at another person's view of the world. This involves taking into account a situation existing at the present time without reflection on a person's past history.

Among the other factors in Hegelian philosophy, which are relevant to the plot of the novel, is the notion that there is the desire in self-consciousness to destroy in some way, or actually kill, another person if he or she is an obstruction to its fulfilment. For this reason, Beauvoir undoubtedly included the murder of the protagonist, Xavière, at the end of the plot, even though she later expressed regrets with regard to this final scenario. She felt that the ending was aesthetically disastrous and that Françoise was, in reality, as incapable as herself in committing such an act.[23] However, in literary terms, and in line with the fulfilment of existentialist desire, the story ends with the elimination of a person in the love triangle who represents a major problem for the main protagonist, Françoise.

The development of the plot is seen through the eyes of this main protagonist. As a parallel, Beauvoir recounts her life experiences through her: the meeting with Olga Kosakievicz and life with Jean-Paul Sartre. Although biographical details are changed, they reflect the creation of love/death figurative language used in the novel via the framework of existentialist convictions and Hegelian philosophy. These led to the use of death-like feelings in love and jealousy such as "funeral shades", "poisoned atmosphere" and "black and torrid lava".

Other origins in the symbolisation of love as a form of death will now be explored in Hesse's writing. Two biographical threads in Hesse's life will be briefly taken up here. One concerns the contemporary Freudian approach, prevalent at that time, to his personal make-up, and the other is directly linked to his inner psychological torments.

8.8 Freudian Psychology in Hermann Hesse

Hermann Hesse was born around the same time as D. H. Lawrence, the former a little earlier in 1877 and the latter in 1885. To a certain extent, they were therefore contemporaries, except that Hesse, like Beauvoir, lived a lot longer. His date of death was 1962. Comparing the dates of the lives of the three authors, Beauvoir thus lived at a slightly later period, but all three were influenced by events which occurred in the first half of the 20th century. The Freudian life and death instinct, discussed earlier, undoubtedly played a part in the works of both Hesse and Lawrence, but for reasons which were, to some extent, divergent.

Two similarities in their lives were, on the one hand, the social customs surrounding Hesse with its conformist views and, on the other, the disastrous effect of the Great War. In the first case, social customs were a little different to Lawrence due to the fact that Hesse lived, like Beauvoir, in a very bourgeois society. He found it stifling in its "comfortable" and "traditional" way. In the second case of the war, he felt that the ultra "technical and rational" environment of the contemporary world, with its catastrophes and impending wars, threatened humanity.[24] This latter point undoubtedly plays a major role in the protagonist, Haller, in *Steppenwolf* and his "trip through hell".

The two factors were underscored by the ongoing psychological torment within Hesse from an early age. Even at the age of 14, he had thoughts of suicide. A year later, he attempted to commit suicide, which resulted in his being sent to a psychiatric institution. After having spent some time in psychiatric care, he deeply criticised his father and the "artificial" nature of the Pietist Protestantism in which he grew up. Following an apprenticeship as a mechanic, he finally turned to literature. In 1904, he married Maria Bennoulli who, to a large extent, psychologically resembled him.

After these initial years, his contact with Freudian psychology began with a period of psychiatric treatment following a difficult period of time in his life. This included the death of his father, the illness of his youngest child and a crisis in his marriage. In 1916, Hesse began psychiatric therapy with Bernhard Lang who was a disciple of Freud. Hesse also became a close friend of Lang, and as a result of 60 sessions during the course of that year, he began to overcome the innermost emotional crises he had been through since early childhood. He maintained, in line with Freudian psychology, that after searching for the mental causes arising from memories and dreams, a "passionate and warm feeling" can fluctuate between the conscious and unconscious.[25]

The similarities between Hesse's life and *Steppenwolf* are very apparent. First, the names of the main protagonists: Harry Haller and Hermann Hesse, both of whose names begin with H. H., as well as Maria in the novel and the Maria of Hesse's first wife. In short, Hesse recounts his feelings through the character of Haller. The events which lead up to the writing of this scenario are briefly as follows.

In the period before the publication of *Steppenwolf* in 1927, Hesse suffered deeply, as outlined above, from three main social factors: first, the chaos of wars; second, the bourgeois world which he tried to avoid during this period; and third, an increasingly technological world of machines in industry and in the urban or rural landscape which he felt were created for their own sake. In addition, Hesse undertook another series of psychiatric therapy at the time, suffering as ever from the attempt to understand the cleavage between his inner emotions and the chaotic world around him.

This scenario is undoubtedly reflected in the character of Haller in the novel. The essence of the plot is that, in order to understand the cleavage, he needs to make a "trip through hell" with the aim of penetrating the unconsciousness of his "magical ego". This is essential since he cannot simply avoid, or deviate in some form or other, from the chaos of the world he is living in. The trip takes place in the magical theatre towards the end of the book, in which his past life is reflected in mirrors. The result of this experience is that he realises reality can only be found within oneself. Haller does not find the ideal solution to the problem, but the trip in no way ends in despair or tragedy. On the contrary, a higher plane of conceptualisation arises above the chaos: a more positive, universal world which represents a stage in the theatre untouched by the "barbaric civilisations" that surround the protagonist. The stage offers a forum in which deity and the spirit can talk to humanity, far from the barbaric world. Furthermore, a symbol of hope acts as a guiding light through the frightening effects of the trip: Haller looks for a sign or a word which leads to hope and immortality, such as "the sun", and he finds the word: MOZART.[26] The concept of music introduces a meaning to life. The sign is undoubtedly linked to Hesse's upbringing in classical music.

The fact of coming to terms with the schizophrenic, psychological make-up of Haller can be linked to Hesse's similar ambivalent attitude towards love which was discussed in the previous chapter. The ambivalence ranges between the metaphoric abyss of the barbaric world to the constellations of hope. On this note, the preceding discussions of LOVE IS DEATH have undoubtedly tended towards the notion of MORTALITY. In a logical sense, mortality represents death since the latter signifies the end of life in some form or other. However, the conceptualisation of death can also move towards the opposite direction of IMMORTALITY.

8.9 *Real and Non-Real Worlds*

The notion of immortality raises the issue of real and non-real (or fantasy) worlds. So far, the discussions on figurative language have concerned the real world of protagonists in literary discourse. It has been argued that this real world in fiction has also been projected from the real world of the author. The poems about the epidemic in chapter 1 use figurative language to describe real-world events. The protagonists in the works of Lawrence, Beauvoir and Hesse live in real-world scenarios. Conceptual mapping has therefore dealt with reality using figurative language.

More intricate types of mapping evolve from the interchange between real and non-real worlds. The borderline between the two is sometimes difficult to define. In the mind of the writer, the literal concepts of the real world can merge into fantasy concepts of a non-real world. Literal meaning is usually founded on the basis of worldly knowledge. The preceding discussions on mappings have concerned the logical assumption of death being mapped onto mortality. In rather innovative ways, this can be the case of love, particularly when a love affair in certain circumstances is conceived as an impossible venture or scenario. However, death can also be symbolised as an immortal concept, as at the end of *Steppenwolf* mentioned above.

A survey of comparative literature reveals that a trend towards immortality becomes apparent with a notion such as time. An underlying base mapping like DEATH IS TIME can portray both mortality and immortality, according to the mindset of an author. Again, a wide interpretation of the mapping is needed, as in LOVE IS DEATH. For example, death may represent someone dying or a deceased person from the recent or distant past. Time may be close or distant to the present point in time, as well as finite or infinite.

In order to distinguish real and non-real worlds in fiction, as well as the projection from biographical sources, the death/time equation will be taken up here. This entails a DEATH IS TIME framework of conceptualisation, which can be used to examine the notion of reality. Multiple conceptual mapping is set up according to real and non-real worlds. They may occur in both the actual world of an author or in fiction. The real world may depend on the perception of such features as scientific facts or beliefs and may interchange with a fantasy world. In this way, mental spaces and discourse worlds, truth values and reference all become extremely flexible.

The six-tier model in the search for origins in the figurative language of literary discourse has so far involved tracing words back from (1) the language used; (2) the conceptualisation of figurative thought; (3) the cultural history of words; (4) the contextual reference of mappings at level one; (5) figurative language in the narratives of comparative literature and (6) the personal biographies of authors,

(Level 2 reference), which instigate scenarios leading to the final words in their writing.

In order to see how the DEATH IS TIME model operates in the natural order of linguistic production, the process will again be reversed by proceeding from level (1) to level (6), as in chapter 1. Before starting out on this procedure in relation to death, the cognitive approach will be taken up again with regard to exploring the ways the human mind conceptualises time. The next chapter will therefore enter the realm of mapping by taking into account possible real and non-real worlds.

Notes

1 Messud (2018).
2 Leyris, *Le Monde* (08/06/2018). Illusions perçues.
3 Garner, *The New York Times* (21/08/2017). 'The Burning Girl', About Intense Pre-Teenage Friendship Never Catches Fire.
4 Wimsatt and Beardsley (1946, 1949).
5 Rabatel (2014, 2015).
6 Doubrovsky (1977).
7 Proust [1919] (2013).
8 Jenny (2003).
9 Pillière (2013: 7).
10 Dion and Regard (2013).
11 Booth (1999), citing the Cambridge University Press biography of Lawrence: Ellis, ed. (1998).
12 idem.: 462.
13 Friedman (2000: 207).
14 Marnat (1966: 47–48).
15 *The Guardian* (18/08/1914). "A War of Machines".
16 Bell (2015: para. 6).
17 idem.: 207.
18 Both claims can be found in Growse (2012).
19 Moi (1994).
20 idem. (1995: 63ff.).
21 Lukavská (1977).
22 Op. cit. Moi (1995: 186ff.).
23 idem. (1995: 146).
24 Zeller (1963: 100).
25 idem.: 76.
26 idem.: 100–102.

9 Conceptualisation of the Real World

9.1 Time Trajectories in Literal Meaning

In order to establish how time is normally conceptualised in a real world according to cognitive views of perception, the following discussion suggests that time is usually perceived as a unidirectional, linear paradigm with a beginning and an end. Time is a constant; it cannot accelerate or slow down, and it is usually observed from a deictic viewpoint.

It should be pointed out here that conceptualisation can, in certain circumstances, change according to worldly knowledge. In chapter 6, it was seen that the Ancient Greeks' conceptualisation of the planet Venus in terms of two Gods defined their source of symbolism. Another more modern observation is the scientific fact of time dilation. This occurs in Einstein's Theory of Relativity with regard to an object travelling at a very fast speed in outer space. It has been proved a number of times and modern-day evidence for it can be seen in GPS measurements taken by satellites in orbit around the Earth. This notion of time is extremely difficult to comprehend from the point of view on Earth, and the literary genre of science fiction has constantly attempted to come to terms with it. One of the most well-known works which has combined time dilation with a science-fiction scenario is Pierre Boule's novel, *La planète des singes* (1963) and its Hollywood production, Planet of the Apes (1968). As a result, even the real world of science may cause fluctuations in the conceptualisation of time paradigms. The one permanent feature of these changing conditions seems to be that the human mind, as in the case of language, appears to continue observing scientific phenomena from a deictic centre.

DOI: 10.4324/9781032130378-9

Time is often viewed in spatial terms, such as in a TIME IS SPACE conceptual metaphor, although this is not always the case. Verb tenses in Indo-European languages, for example, are usually conceptualised within spatial orientation. They take into account the observer's position with the past being behind the interlocutor and the future in front: "I have put this difficult episode behind me" or "I am looking forward to a brighter future". A major feature of temporal syntax is that there is an A to B movement in which the past remains in the past and vice versa for the future.

As a result, linguistic structures are based on deictic perception, whereby verbal conjugations follow sequential ordering of earlier and later time dimensions in line with the different types of past and future tenses. This framework has been developed along the lines of six time dimensions in English cognitive grammar. Perfect tenses are defined as "anterior" and progressive tenses as "posterior". The linear structure of the verb "to go" would therefore progress chronologically through six time zones from the most distant past, "had gone" as past anterior to the most distant future, "will have been going", as future posterior.[1] However, a feature to be emphasised here is that the notion of "anterior" implies a backward-looking direction for actions which have already finished, regardless of whether the time is in the past or future, and likewise "posterior" is forward-looking. It can be deduced that the reason for this cognitive perception is due to the deictic reference point.

In addition to this basic pattern, a variation occurs in the division between what has been termed "ego- and non-ego-centred conceptualisation".[2] Although these represent separate entities, it may be argued that they both have a deictic base. Ego-centred time implies that the observer progresses along the time-line, whereas a non-ego pattern, often referred to as "time-moving", implies that the observer is in a fixed position and events move around the deixis. This distinction has been further divided into perspective-specific and perspective-neutral models.[3] The first refers to the two patterns of ego-related specifications. The second highlights the aspect of time location being relative to other times, and not specifically to the observer's position. In other words, they operate independently of any considerations regarding the ego parameter, as in the expression, "a reception followed the talks". These variations are equally based on a linear structure in which events always progress towards the future. Either the observer moves forward or events around the deictic position move forward in relation to other circumstances.

Conceptualisation of the Real World 91

Cognitive studies have also proposed models of time which lay less emphasis on a linear effect and more on the fact that such circumstances are blended together. One of the major alternative theories in this field is that of blended mental spaces mentioned in chapter 5. In this case, blends represent particular events, which also incorporate a starting point and destination. Observers and their circumstances move together, while objects are aligned according to fixed relative positions. One of the arguments for this theory is the phenomenon of causal relations: events lead from one situation to another due to causal effects. It can be deduced from these claims that the conceptualisation of time, with a starting and finishing point, necessarily implies a unidirectional format. Duration and direction of these models automatically envisage limits in time within a linear scenario.

The linguistic distinction between ego- and non-ego-centred conceptualisation in grammar is a clear one. The latter is similar to the notion of deictic projection in literature. In other words, our viewpoint can be shifted to see things as specific characters do in literary discourse. In spatial terms, these may include phrases like "on your left" or "it's behind you". These deictic elements go beyond space; they also include a relational aspect to participants in the text such as how they are socially related to each other.[4]

In the last analysis, however, it could be argued that both ego and non-ego conceptualisation is ultimately related to a deictic base. Even an expression, such as "a reception followed the talks", uses a past verbal form, which is related to the observer's position. If the verb "follow" was in the future, it would refer to future time of the observer's position, even if the subject of the sentence is not actually the observer. Deictic projection here is initially from an ego-centred source. Other forms of time/space conceptualisation, which are represented by different cultures, also tend to exhibit an ego-centred, or deictic, position at their base.

9.2 Multicultural Conceptualisation of Time and Space

The linear structure of time can vary. In literary discourse, a cyclic direction can be seen, for example, in certain poetic settings. The same applies to random direction. However, directions of this kind reinforce the idea of movement from one point to another without going backwards or forwards in time. The deictic position moves spatially but not temporally, as in the vampire in Karen Russell's short story, Vampires in the Lemon Grove[5]: "I once pictured time as a black magnifying glass and myself as a microscopic, flightless insect trapped in that circle of night". Here, the motion of the trapped insect is either circular or random rather than linear, representing an image of enclosure or encirclement. It is, in fact, an attempt to conceptualise time, not with duration but with movement in an enclosed notion of space.

Many Western models of linear time are represented by other spatial paradigms. The cyclic pattern can be observed in the Toba language of Bolivia.[6] Time passes in a counter clockwise direction in relation to the observer: the present is in front, the recent past to the left, the distant past behind and the future on the right-hand side. The point here is that the space behind the observer could represent both the distant past and the future when time moves around to the right. Other similar variants of time and space, from a diachronic point of view, could be cited such as the cyclic pattern in the classical Mayan calendar or the Western (Gregorian) system. The latter has a linear representation of time mapped onto a cyclic structure denoting motion from an origin (the birth of Christ) to a notional endpoint (the end of Days).[7] However, certain aspects become apparent in all of these systems in real-world conceptualisation. First, there is a notion of time limits. Space is allocated to a particular time; there is the pattern of a beginning and an end and the passing of time tends to be unidirectional. Second, it is also deictic and limited to time constraints: the observer's position does not go back into the past. Likewise, there is a destination in the future: the end of a journey or experience implies finite time.

Time trajectories, as in the theories mentioned above, thus reflect conceptualisation within a literal-meaning framework of a real world. In a nutshell, it has been suggested that Western society, whose image of people living in a certain time and space and no more, reveals a "linear and closure-oriented, spatio-temporal trajectory within perfectly closed spatial configurations, predicating a unidirectional, linear, teleological temporality progressively moving towards completion".[8] In the world of literature, this view of time is easily transformed. The real world now moves toward the border with the fantasy world and other forms of conceptual mapping in figurative language.

9.3 Time and Space in Literary Thought

It has been suggested that time trajectories, particularly in postmodernist literature, abandons standard patterns reflected in literal thought. Time becomes multidimensional and unstable in narrative texts:

In consciousness, and, hence, in the text as its product, the category of time has a more difficult structure, a wider range and a more voluminous, unreal plane. The literary world represents a complex, multiplane construction with a narrative structure and a story line, where the objective characteristics of time are transformed. Time becomes unsteady, diverse and reversible. Text time (story time, the time of narration) is multidimensional and discrete, retrospective and prospective, unsteady and unstable. Shifts in time also cause shifts in space which is reflected in M. Bakhtin's theory about chronotope, as a unity of time and space.[9]

In the light of spatio-temporal trajectories in cognitive theories and the multidimensional aspect of time in narrative, a number of examples have been proposed as to how death is conceptualised in the form of metaphors in both everyday language and literature. One spatial construct of death involves the DEATH IS GOING TO A FINAL DESTINATION conceptual metaphor.[10] In other words, death involves spatial displacement as in the following poem:

> How gladly would I meet
> Mortality, my sentence, and be earth
> Insensible! How glad would lay me down
> As in my mother's lap!
> *Paradise Lost, Book 10*, John Milton

The return to earth and to the mother's lap signifies, in many ways, a cyclic movement within a closed spatial configuration. Cognitive examples such as these point out equally the notions of departure, sleep and rest. A direct mapping with death being mapped onto time in general is less salient. However, the present study reveals that, at least symbolically, death is often mapped onto time and, in many cases, within the parameter of space. Time generally has either a finite dimension or an infinite one. In other words, it can refer to mortality, as in the example above, or immortality. This contrasts with love being mapped onto death; the latter tends to infer a finite, and therefore impossible, dimension of love.

Infinity in symbolic time enters a new dimension, similar to the discovery of time dilation in literal thought, when figurative language comes into play. As suggested above with regard to postmodernist literature, the deictic position can move forwards or backwards in time and space. The aspect of infinity may be conceived in a purely

94 *Conceptualisation of the Real World*

unidirectional movement forwards, if the life-to-death pattern is taken more symbolically as a progression from mortality to eternity in accordance with religious views.[11] However, the following discussions will propose that deictic, infinite movement in time may be both forward and backwards. This may also depend on the notion of beliefs with regard to the real world.

9.4 Conceptualisation and Beliefs in Emily Dickinson

The borderline between the real and non-real world automatically raises this issue of beliefs. One mindset may be based on scientific worldly knowledge. Another may depend on an aspect such as religious belief. It could be argued that a religious framework for the conceptualisation of infinity, for example, represents the "real world" for the observer.

An illustration of infinity in the temporal dimension of mappings, according to the notion of religious belief, will first be illustrated by the poetry of Emily Dickinson. An insight into the background of novelists and poets will be the starting point. The assumption is therefore that biographies again play a major role and that this background may be used to determine the type of figurative discourse produced by writers.

Emily Dickinson (1830–1886) was brought up in a strict Protestant environment in the 19th century region of New England in the United States. The religious side of her beliefs is revealed in her poetry and explains the use of her poetic descriptions of eternity and death. Indeed, the two concepts are important in many of her poems. She led a very reclusive life in the family home, her main contact with people on the outside being in the form of written correspondence. Her solitary existence no doubt contributed to her deep reflections on life and death, although the possible causes of isolating herself from society, ranging from social anxiety to agoraphobia, remain largely speculative.

One particular analytical framework, among the different works of literary criticism published about her poems, is the notion of *self-reflexiveness*. It will be discussed here with regard to her conceptualisation of the world around her. It has been defined as "the human ability to pay attention to what we pay attention to by moving to a higher order of abstracting, our power to develop a detached almost third-person perspective about a first-person perspective".[12] According to this view, Dickinson was one of the most self-reflexive poets in American literature with regard to difficult human experience

Conceptualisation of the Real World 95

such as pain, shock and suffering. This can be seen in her poem, *After Great Pain, a Formal Feeling Comes*.[13]

> After great pain, a formal feeling comes –
> The Nerves sit ceremonious, like Tombs –
> The stiff Heart questions 'was it He, that bore,'
> And 'Yesterday, or Centuries before'?
> The Feet, mechanical, go round –
> A Wooden way
> Of Ground, or Air, or Ought –
> Regardless grown,
> A Quartz contentment, like a stone –

The interpretation here is that the poet becomes aware of a numb acceptance of her previously sharp and intense pain as a reaction to shock. Nerves are transformed into metaphoric tombs and her feet into different materials of wood, quartz or stone.[14] It could be deduced from the process of self-reflexiveness that conceptualisation can detach itself from a current state of affairs into another realm of imagery. In this case, numbness is depicted by inert objects and, in certain cases, with a reference to death and timelessness. In other terms, the ego is transferred from the emotional world of pain to a fantasy world of mortality. With regard to mental spaces and time/space theories outlined above, the deictic point of the observer is thereby projected from one sub-world to another.

The step from mortality to eternity is illustrated by other poems such as the first and last verses of *Because I could not stop for Death*[15]:

> Because I could not stop for Death -
> He kindly stopped for me -
> The Carriage held but just Ourselves -
> And Immortality
> Since then –'tis Centuries – and yet
> Feels shorter than the Day
> I first surmised the Horses' Heads
> Were toward Eternity

According to her religious beliefs, a new aspect of time trajectories is introduced in this scenario. The after-life continues indefinitely without a temporal or spatial finishing point. The notion of eternity displaces the deictic position to a point in time beyond mortality. Duration has no meaning: centuries have passed, but the lapse of time could have been one day. The conceptual process thus transfers the observer's position to a time zone in which the poet's own funeral is situated in the past. The verses of the poem demonstrate how the personification of the death symbol operates within the context of a funeral carriage. As a result, it leads the observer to eternity.

It can therefore be seen that the conceptualisation of time moves into a new dimension, in the same way as time dilation requires a new dimension of perception. Eternity appears to be the real world of Emily Dickinson. However, although both examples mirror the real world according to the observer's position – time dilation corresponds to new astrophysical laws and the after-life is a true fact in the eyes of the religious believer - the mental process of time perception is different. In the first case, the real world is based on science; in the second, it is based on religious belief. However, it may be claimed that both dimensions are construed according to the conceptualisation of a real world in the eyes of the observer.

On the basis of foregoing theories on the origins of figurative language, it may be deduced that a cognitive analysis of Dickinson's poetry, starting at the origins themselves, can be seen in the following steps. The analysis of her poetry is based on an adapted cognitive framework put forward here.

First, at the biographical level, the poet wishes to express her thoughts on the after-life due to her religious beliefs and family environment. This is linked to her preoccupations about the theme of death which arises frequently in her poetry. Second, and at the narrative level, the context of the poem, *Because I could not stop for Death,* reveals that the scenario is a funeral which provides information about the symbolic imagery in the poem. Third, the referential point of figurative language is the poet herself, portrayed by the pronoun "*I*" in the first line. It can therefore be inferred that Dickinson herself imagines she is at her own funeral and it is her own after-life. Fourth, the cultural-historical level can be seen in the use of the horse and carriage at the funeral. Although these concepts, or from a semiotic point of view of signs, could refer to other times in history, the 19th century setting is a poignant one for indicating the symbolic direction of the horses' heads. Motorised funeral hearses of the 21st century could not be used. Fifth, one construal of a conceptual metaphor in cognition is the mapping DEATH IS UNLIMITED TIME. This is a more specific mapping from the basic DEATH IS TIME metaphor proposed above. Through the use of figurative thought, the overall message of the poem is that the after-life signifies eternity. Another important figurative process is, of course, the personification of Death which stops the funeral carriage to pick up the poet. Finally, the actual words used in the poem in a symbolic sense are, apart from Death, the horses and carriage. As mentioned above, the horses' heads are directed towards eternity and the carriage itself contains three concepts: Death, the poet and eternity. The words "horses" and "carriage" are therefore used as symbols of eternity in the figurative language of the poem. The preceding analysis gives a very brief breakdown of how the poet presumably came to write this short poem with the origins in her personal biography and preoccupation of death.

Until now, it can be seen that a real world for a writer may be based on scientific facts or on beliefs. Changes in conceptualisation may depend on evolving scientific knowledge or beliefs. The first comes to terms with changes in standard theory such as the speed of time. The second sees a real world in which immortality exists: the soul continues forever. The move towards immortality in death, according to the second example, appears to adopt the six-tier model of metaphor origins based on a real-life scenario. In other words, the analysis of Dickinson's poetry suggests that her belief in the after-life is the starting point for her linguistic use of symbolism. Although there is a transformation from a stage of life to the after-life, it appears to be a natural evolution of events, whatever happens.

Conceptualisation of a non-real, or fantasy, world arguably involves a different mental process. The writer intentionally changes real-world possibilities to non-real features in the scenario. This may be for any number of personal reasons. It could be simply an imaginative world in science-fiction literature, but it may also contain specific messages or reveal personal dilemmas in the search for particular solutions to existence. In all the ways, various mapping processes become apparent. A transformation of reality may begin at the start of a literary piece of work or at some stage during the scenario itself. On this basis, the next stage will be to explore the creation of fantasy worlds and their use of figurative language. The discussion will turn to some fascinating examples in South American literature.

Notes

1 Radden (2003: 201ff).
2 Boroditsky (2000).
3 Moore (2006).
4 Stockwell (2002: 43-44).
5 Russel (2014).
6 Op. cit. Radden (2003: 6).

7 Sinha et al. (2011).
8 Vukanović and Grmuša (2009: 11).
9 Fedosova (2015: 81).
10 Lakoff and Turner (1989: 14–15).
11 Ibid.: 11.
12 Maas (2003).
13 Dickinson [1890] (2003: 181).
14 Op.cit. Maas (2003).
15 Dickinson [1890] (1998).

10 The Transformation of Reality

10.1 The Venezuelan Poet Eugenio Montejo

One particular writer in South American literature, who was interested in the notion of time, is the late Venezuelan poet, essayist, editor and diplomat, Eugenio Montejo (1938–2008). An aspect of time in his poetry is the association between self-identity and personal environment, a feature which can be seen in many of his works. He was also particularly interested in the concept of death. A fundamental issue relates to how the present can be linked up to the past and future. In his poetry, time dimensions of the past and future become intermingled. On this basis, observers and events move by switching between the past and future. Memories and conjectures along the time dimension provide a catalyst to investigate the mysteries of life and existence. Although Montejo was not a strong religious believer in the same way as Dickinson, one interpretation of his poetry could be that he was looking for a certain kind of spirituality in his life which would help explain the enigmatic concept of life and death.

Montejo was born in the capital city of Caracas and grew up at a time when substantial changes were taking place in the country. One particular example was the fact that the Venezuelan economy was changing from a predominantly agricultural one to an oil-exporting country. Fundamental changes such as these had a large influence on his life. Indeed, the transformation of familiar objects and events in his environment was linked to Montejo's general feelings that changes can create continual temporal, spatial, physical and emotional upheavals in an individual's existence. One example of this was that he seemed to be perturbed in his memory of familiar towns, or districts of towns, being demolished to build new types of

DOI: 10.4324/9781032130378-10

unfamiliar urban landscape. The result was that the personal reaction of the writer to the conceptualisation of his surroundings led to personalised notions of concepts, signs and symbols.

This argument is supported by the fact that Montejo grew up in an environment in which he was personally very sensitive to objects and sounds around him – forms of perception which were even more important than words. It was particularly the case with images of nature. This phenomenon has been described in fine detail:

> Montejo, who spent his childhood in touch with the countryside, preferred the sounds of nature – the croaking of frogs, the singing of cicadas, crickets or birds, the sounds of the wind or two bodies in love – to words.[1]

The familiar sounds and objects in his childhood, found in many of his poems, represent a form of loss which Montejo attempts to come to terms with or even avoid in his poetry.[2]

Montejo was also particularly sensitive to memories about the house and immediate surroundings he grew up in. One particular memory was the bakery run by his father where white flour would cover everything on the premises. He describes the effects in an essay "The White Workshop" (*El Taller Blanco*).[3] He uses poignant analogies about white flour which would cover "hair, hands, skin, and also things, gestures and words". On a trip later to Paris in a snow-covered landscape, he was not surprised to see everything covered in white, contrary to the experience of those from the tropics who see snow for the first time.

Such details of his childhood had a profound effect on his memories and subsequently on his poetry. His poetic interest focused to a large extent on the notion of deceased persons within the overall concept of death and how it fitted into time scales. Various reasons have been suggested by literary critics about the poet's approach to time, including the application of space.[4] It appears that Montejo's memories are reflected above all in the memories of deceased persons. He does not live in the past but in the present point of time with the help of a particular memory. It is as if a memory actually represents the present moment. In this way, memories and the present are juxtaposed to create a time dimension which is not weakened by the influence of what might be termed 'reality' or the 'real world'. Deceased members of the family thereby live in a present dimension of time recreated by memory so that death provides a convenient meeting place for Montejo and his family. It is almost as if his memories represent a borderline between reality and non-reality.

It has also been suggested that the fusion of time implies another notion of space. The signs and symbols of memory, such as walls, windows and so on, establish a new spatial form whereby perception mingles with mental projection. The original sign, which is fixed in memory, becomes a different projection of thoughts on the part of the observer, and recreates new human forms. All objects and events become a network of relationships that are continually recreated in memory to produce new scenarios. The locations of original signs are thus conceptually changed. The outcome of this conceptualisation is that Montejo constructs a symbolic universe in which each sign, intermingled with an infinite multiplication of forms, forges one basic unit: the search for the origins and destiny of his own personal existence. According to this view, the perception of time in memory represents Montejo's search to come to terms with the mystery of death, and likewise his quest for a form of spirituality which is born from the world of memories.

10.2 Transfigured Time

Despite the borderline of reality and non-reality in his memories, Montejo takes a deliberate step in changing the notion of time.[5] One poem which represents the idea illustrated above and an intentional change is *Tiempo transfigurado,* or "Transfigured Time".[6] The intentional act of changing time gives the impression of a non-real world.

Tiempo transfigurado	*Transfigured time*
A António Ramos Rosa	To António Ramos Rosa
La casa donde mi padre va a nacer no está concluida, le falta una pared que no han hecho mis manos.	The house where my father will be born is still unfinished, it lacks a wall my hands have not yet built.
Sus pasos, que ahora me buscan por la tierra, vienen hacia esta calle.	His footsteps searching for me across the earth now comes towards this street.
No logro oílos, todavía no me alcanzan.	Yet I can't hear them, they still don't reach me.
Detrás de aquella puerta se oyen ecos y voces que a leguas reconozco, pero son dichas por los retratos.	Behind that door are echoes and voices I recognize miles off, but they are spoken only by portraits.
El rostro que no se ve en ningún espejo porque tarda en nacer o ya no existe, puede ser de cualquiera de nosotros - a todos se parece.	The face not seen in any mirror, because it's late being born or still doesn't exist, could be any one of us – it look like all of us.

(Continued)

Tiempo transfigurado	Transfigured time
En esa tumba no están mis huesos sino los del bisnieto Zacarías, que usaba bastón y seudónimo Mis restos ya se perdieron.	My bones are not in that tomb but those of Zacarias, the great-grandson, who used a walking-stick and pseudonym. My own remains have long been lost.
Esta poema escrito en otro siglo, por mí, por otro, no recuerdo, alguna noche junto a un cabo de vela.	This poem was written in another century, by me, by someone else, I don't recall some night by a guttering candle.
El tiempo dio cuenta de la llama y entre mis manos quedó a oscuras sin haberlo leído.	Time consumed the flame and lingered in my darkened hands and in these eyes that never read the poem.
Cuando vuelva a alumbrar ya estaré ausente.	When the candle returns with its light I'll already be gone.

(Translation: Peter Boyle)

10.3 Time Symbolism and Language Structure

It will be suggested here that the syntax of verbal structures in the poem represent symbols in the perception of time. Furthermore, the Spanish original demonstrates that the varied use of the verb 'to be', (*ser/estar*), is a language-specific feature that can be adapted to enhance the present point in time. The double Spanish lexeme, which does not exist in English, is used to attribute qualities and characteristics in the case of *ser*, and temporary conditions or states with regard to *estar*. The latter often refers to an action or state which is in the process of continuing or lasting, and is therefore often translated by the gerund construction of -*ing* in English. However, this is not always possible.

A case in point is in the first verse of the poem with the construction in Spanish: ... *no está concluida*, which has to be reinforced in English by the word "still": "is still unfinished". However, the symbolic emphasis of transferring the construction of the house to the present, when it was actually finished a long time ago, is lost in the English verbal structure since an -*ing form* (being unfinished), is not possible here.

A second example is in the fifth verse with reference to "bones in the tomb": *en esa tumba no están mis huesos*. Since it is not possible to write "my bones are not being in that tomb", it is a case in which the emphasis on an ongoing state in the present cannot be mirrored by the

English verbal system. It can therefore be concluded that, in the same way language-specific morphology can play a part in metaphoric compound nouns, as in the case of D. H. Lawrence, this form of morpho-syntax in verbal structures can be specific to one language in the creation of symbolic images.

Symbolic time transformation is evident and can be summarised in a number of different verb structures and tenses. At the beginning of the poem, it can be seen that an important concept, or sign from a semiotic viewpoint, is the notion of a house in the memory of the poet. It symbolises his childhood and where he grew up. The first incongruent pattern of time, or incongruent in the cognitive sense of the term, is to be seen in the first verse in which it becomes fused between the past and the future: "...where my father will be born... the wall my hands have not yet built". The observer's position is thus placed before future events which, in reality, have already taken place. Furthermore, the perspective is one of the child building a wall for his father when he is born at a later date. The intermingling of past and future continues in the second verse with the father's footsteps which have still not reached the observer. The existence of the father contrasts with the timing of his birth which has not yet taken place.

A second incongruent pattern is the reference to the observer's death in the line mentioned above: "my bones are not in that tomb...", suggesting that his death has already occurred. In that respect, the observer's position in his memories contrasts with the postulated point in time in the past, when he still has to build a wall of the house, with that of the future. The latter is a long way into the future, as in "...but those of Zacarias, the great-grandson (...) my own remains have long been lost". The long period of time, or the notion of eternity, is extended further by the description of the past in the last verse: "This poem was written in another century". This is emphasised by the personification of "Time consumed the flame and lingered in my darkened hands..." Events continue to switch backwards and forwards between the past and future at the end of the poem: "When the candle returns with its light, I'll already be gone".

The Spanish original reflects the anterior and posterior cognitive grammar outlined above, as in: "*va a nacer*" (will be born); "*no han hechos*"(have not yet built), etc. However, the deictic reference point constantly switches between anterior and posterior within the past, present and future time frames by using the same memories. This mechanism operates in the form of signs which appear in the poet's mind such as "house" and other related objects and events. Different descriptions of the house – the wall, the door, the portraits, the mirror – are subordinate signs to the superordinate concept of the house. The latter forms an umbrella term for the memories and events in the place where the poet lived during his childhood. References to the future, although fixed in past memory, are related to the unbuilt wall, the street in which the house is located and the mirror which cannot yet reflect unborn faces. One form of perception of past time is therefore in the portraits of people who are deceased.

10.4 Switching Between Past and Future

From a cognitive point of view, the deictic notion of time perception in the poem is reflected by the observer recounting memories according to his position in time. Even the image of time consuming the flame of the candle is linked to the observer. The description of the "flame lingering in my darkened hands" relates to an ego-centred position. However, the fundamental difference concerns the linear order of temporal sequences: the continual switching backwards and forwards between anterior and posterior positions in the past, present and future. In addition, objects and events keep eternally re-appearing.

Furthermore, there appear to be no borders between temporal units of existence, such as the threshold between life and death. There is no point in time in the poet's memories in which his existence changes from life to death. This form of time conceptualisation, in turn, has an impact on the time – space relationship.

10.5 New Spatial Forms

It has been suggested that the fusion of time implies another notion of space.[7] The signs and symbols of memory, such as walls, windows and so on, establish a new spatial form whereby perception mingles with mental projection. The original sign, which is fixed in memory, becomes a different projection of thoughts on the part of the observer, and re-creates new human forms. All objects and events become a network of relationships that are continually recreated in memory to produce new scenarios. The locations of original signs are thus conceptually changed. The outcome of this conceptualisation is that Montejo constructs a symbolic universe in which each sign, intermingled with an infinite multiplication of forms, forges one basic unit: the search for the origins and destiny of his own personal existence. This perception of time in memory appears to represent Montejo's search in coming to terms with the mystery of death, and likewise his quest for a form of spirituality which is born from the world of memories.[8]

In his poems, and particularly in *Tiempo transfigurado*, the concepts of time and place thereby become mixed and are turned upside down. The border between life and death is erased, the predominantly unidirectional notion of time and existence appears to become obsolete. His ancestors constantly change between life and death. The transformations of familiar objects and events in his memories are linked to Montejo's general feelings that changes in the environment create continual temporal, spatial, physical and emotional upheavals in an individual's existence. As suggested above, this stems from the fact that he was indeed often perturbed by familiar towns, or districts of towns in his memory, being demolished to build new types of unfamiliar urban landscape. The result is that the personal reaction of the poet to the conceptualisation of the environment leads to personalised notions of concepts and signs, as opposed to the more universal theories of time conceptualization proposed in cognitive science.

Along the lines of the six-tier model of origins, the foregoing details reveal that the type of symbolic language used by Montejo appears to fit in with the following phases: first, there is the source of Montejo's personal biography and the fact that he wishes to come to terms in his memories with the loss of deceased persons. Second, the narrative of the poem, *Tiempo transfigurado*, is a journey through Montejo's memories regarding his family members, the house he grew up in and his situation in time as he wrote the poem. Third, the reference point is clearly the poet himself. Fourth, the cultural history and environment is Montejo's childhood in Caracas. Fifth, a figurative mapping, on the basis of a general DEATH IS TIME structure, could be interpreted in the form of DECEASED PERSONS ARE TIME TRANSFORMATION. The memories of deceased persons are therefore transferred to different points on the time scale in a symbolic way. Sixth, the use of the language structure to create symbolism, depends, on the one hand, on verb tenses and, on the other, on lexemes of semiotic signs. The former involves different forms of past, present and future tenses with the language-specific aspects of "to be" suggested above; the latter includes signs such as the house, the portraits on the walls and so on.

10.6 Notions of Real Worlds

The question that arises here is: what is the real world of an author? It can first depend on knowledge of the environment and real events which have occurred. Second, the real world can also relate to beliefs. Third, the distinction of real and non-real worlds may very often be open to interpretation. However, it could be argued that, in

Montejo's case, his real world becomes a fantasy world in his poem. In other words, he intentionally transforms his real world to a form of fantasy within the time dimension. It fits his desire to figuratively meet up with people and periods in his life. The scenario of the poem mentioned above reflects an imaginative world in relation to past and future events.

There are therefore a number of possible conceptual mappings of settings. It may be a real world of an author reflected in a real world of a protagonist. The real world in a scenario may be based on beliefs. Furthermore, a real world may be transformed into a fantasy. The result is that, without attempting to number all possible conceptual mappings available to an author, it is clear that the influence of personal biography may appear in the form of multiple conceptualisation between the so-called real and non-real worlds.

Mappings between sub-worlds also depend on the identity of the author or the protagonists. In some cases, doubts about what constitutes the author's real world are dispelled by clear-cut scenarios. However, multiple conceptualisation originating in personal biography may become more complex due to sub-world interaction that occurs half-way through a narrative. In addition, the author's or protagonist's notion of reality may be ambiguous. The following chapter looks at these aspects of multiple mappings between real and fantasy worlds.

Notes

1 Noguerol (2011: 301).
2 Roberts (2009).
3 Montejo (1996: 127–134). Translation (Peter Boyle): http://www.latinamericanliteraturetoday.org/en/2018/august/white-workshop-eugenio-montejo [accessed: 08/06/2020].
4 Plaza (2007: 13–50).
5 A fuller discussion of Montejo's conceptualisation of time can be found in Trim (2021b).
6 Montejo (2001). Translation (Peter Boyle): https://www.poesi.as/eum1070uk.htm [accessed: 14/02/2020].
7 Op. cit. Plaza (2007).
8 idem. Plaza (2007).

11 Multiple Conceptual Mapping

11.1 The Symbolic Notion of "the South" in Jorge Luis Borges

The foregoing discussions are based on the argument that the initial creation of figurative language in fiction often originates from the author's own life. This may be the projection of his or her own real life onto a "real-life scenario". One example from the literary works analysed is the case of the protagonist, Françoise, in *She Came to Stay*. Her real life in the story undoubtedly reflects Simone De Beauvoir's own life. This fits into a framework which depicts phenomena that are known to us about society, even if the love triangle in the story is normally a non-conventional one. Figurative language, such as the LOVE IS DEATH conceptual metaphor, is based on a real world in the scenario.

Another argument of a "real-life scenario" is observing one's own funeral, as in Dickinson's poem, if there is a strong belief in the after-world. Belief arguably constitutes a real world about our existence. Dickinson probably believed that the scenario could be a real event according to her own beliefs. This argumentation changes in Montejo's poem. His transformation of time cannot logically be a real world in his intentional changes and desires. On the foregoing analysis, it seems to be a fantasy world, even though it could be open to interpretation.

The potential for this type of transformation from a real to fantasy world can lead to multiple mappings. The following discussion is not an exhaustive list of all possibilities but demonstrates some of the scenarios that can occur. They lead to various types of conceptual metaphor and symbol. In addition, they may be interpreted in different

DOI: 10.4324/9781032130378-11

ways by the reader. For example, an obviously real world to the author may be construed as a fantasy world to the reader.

One specific symbol, *the South*, will be examined in the light of such a fantasy world. This type of transformation process is often at the roots of symbolic or figurative writing in general. *The South* is the title of a short story by Jorge Luis Borges (*El Sur*), which he suggested is perhaps his best one.[1] Borges also felt that the story could either be read as a simple narrative or the reader could go much deeper into the story-line. Interpretation about real or non-real worlds is therefore left up to the reader. A brief summary of the plot may be outlined as follows.

The main protagonist, Juan Dahlmann, who works as a secretary in a library in Buenos Aires, obtains a copy of *The Arabian Nights* and rushes home to read it. In his haste, he badly cuts his head on a window frame left open when he runs up the stairs. The result is that he becomes very ill with a high fever due to the accident and is finally sent to hospital. His stay in an anonymous room of the hospital is a horrifying experience for him, causing feelings of humiliation and self-hatred.

After days of suffering, he is finally discharged after almost dying of sepsis. He has a ranch in what is called " the South" and decides to set off there in order to convalesce. When he takes the train for the journey south, the train conductor informs him that the train will not be stopping at his planned destination but only at the station before it. He therefore gets off at this station, which is deserted, and makes his way to a nearby general store where he can get something to eat. He orders food and starts reading *The Arabian Nights*.

Three local farm hands, or *gauchos*, in the store start pestering him and the store-keeper tells him to pay no attention to them as they are drunk. This has the opposite effect on Dahlmann who decides to face up to them. When one of the farm hands pulls out a knife, a customer in the room throws a dagger at Dahlmann's feet to defend himself. Dahlmann now realises he will definitely have to fight the farm hands. He feels he does not stand much of a chance since he has never fought with a knife before. However, he thinks his death will be an honourable one which he would have preferred to a death incurred by sepsis during his stay in hospital. This feeling is reinforced by the fact that he is proud of his grandfather who died while fighting the Catriel Indians in the Pampas of the south.

11.2 The Background to Borges' Life

There are some significant parallel features between the protagonist's life and Borges' own background (Borges was born in Buenos Aires in 1899 and died in Geneva in 1986). Among them are the links to Borges' ancestors in southern Argentina, his work in a library in Buenos Aires and, above all, the fact that he had also suffered a very bad wound to his head which resulted in blood poisoning. The autobiographical or semi-autobiographical aspects of the story have been emphasised by the film director, Carlos Saura, in his TV film, *El Sur*.[2] On the basis of this biographical background, the possibility of going deeper into the story than just following the narrative, as Borges refers to in his introduction, may be centred on the symbol of "The South". Dahlmann's real world in hospital becomes a fantasy story which ends with the knife duel. Fantasy is indeed a major feature of Borges' works with the use of symbols such as mirrors and labyrinths conjuring up imaginative scenarios of the real world.

On this basis, the following discussion will propose a multiple conceptual mapping process linked to the origins of figurative language. In this particular case, the figurative feature of symbolism will be the focus of the model. It involves a projection, first of all, of concepts from the writer's mind that are based on personal experience or general biographical facts. This primary step constitutes a mapping from a biographical source domain to a real-world setting of a protagonist in a given narrative. The second step features a projection from the real world of the protagonist to a fantasy world which he or she creates in the mind. These two steps involve the creation of figurative words from predominant symbols in the story.

11.3 Narratological Conceptual Mappings

The steps are reflected in mappings in the following way. Aspects of Borges' personal experience are mapped onto the real world of Dahlmann. The latter creates a fantasy world on the basis of his own real world in the plot. The fantasy world is represented in conceptual symbols such as the copy of *The Arabian Nights* or the geographical area of "the South".

The latter symbol is an individual creation on the part of Borges but linked to the part of his life in Buenos Aires. It geographically defines the cultural concept of Argentina as starting on the "other side of the Rivadavia main avenue in Buenos Aires": "Everyone knows that the South begins on the other side of the Rivadavia".[3] This avenue is one of the major east – west thoroughfares running through the heart of the city. In Borges' view, crossing the street means entering an "older and more established world". When Dahlmann leaves the hospital to set off on his journey to the South, he symbolically has to cross the street into this other world.

Furthermore, the South represents for Dahlmann a link to his Argentinian ancestry, despite the fact he is also of German descent. It is associated with a ranch he had managed to keep, together with its memories of a pink-coloured building and surrounding eucalyptus trees. The South therefore stands for a memorable and sentimental past. A number of meanings could be interpreted from this symbol on the basis of the CMT framework discussed in chapter three. As a part of figurative thought, metaphor could be substituted for symbol in this particular case, so that one conceptual symbolic mapping may be construed as THE SOUTH IS THE (SENTIMENTAL) PAST. Along the time dimension, the orientation to the south is thus associated with the past. Within this mapping are secondary associations; not only semiotic signs such as the house and eucalyptus trees but also proud memories of his grandfather who died fighting the Catriel Indians. The latter conjures up a romantic past linked to the "romantic" death of his grandfather.[4]

On this basis, the narrative can go much deeper in its reading and, instead of Dahlmann simply being discharged from hospital, he actually remains there in a life-threatening condition. He feels that, compared to the "noble" death of his grandfather, his death from sepsis in hospital will be far less noble. He therefore seeks a way out and creates a fantasy world to make his death resemble that of his grandfather and therefore a more glorious one. The transformation from a real-to-fantasy world is recounted in two particular scenes of the story.

In the first one, the situation in the hospital very quickly worsens and Dahlmann feels as if he is in hell. This is particularly the case after an x-ray examination. Time becomes infinite: "eight days went by but they could have been eight centuries". The result is that he begins to hate himself: his own identity, the humiliation he suffers from being so ill, the difficulties arising from everyday physical needs and so on. However, he does not have time to think about something as abstract as death and, one day, the surgeon tells him he would soon be able to convalesce at his ranch.

In the second scene, Dahlmann's life is quickly transformed into a positive one after this news. He suddenly finds himself in a taxi on the way to Constitution Avenue, another east – west thoroughfare in Buenos Aires. The cooler autumn air, after the hot summer months, were like natural symbols rescuing him from death and fever. This scene finally leads him onto the crossing of the Rivadavia and into his world of fantasy:

Multiple Conceptual Mapping 111

The physical suffering and dark thoughts of his sleepless nights had not given him enough time to think about something as abstract as death. On another day, the surgeon told him he was recovering and, very soon, he would be able to convalesce at his ranch. Incredibly, the promised day arrived.

Reality likes symmetry and slight anachronisms; Dahlmann had arrived at the clinic in a taxi and now a taxi was taking him to the *Constitución*. The first days of cool autumn weather, after the heat of the summer, were like a natural symbol of his destiny which had snatched him from death and fever.

The fantasy world thus begins: the train journey leading to the final scene in the storyline at the general store. Dahlmann creates a scenario in which he dies in the noble way he wishes. He knows that, when he goes out to fight in the open with the farm hands, a noble death will liberate him. The narrative is filled with parallel associations between the clinic and the knife duel, such as being stabbed and having an injection:

They went out, and if Dahlmann felt there was no hope, he wasn't afraid either. He thought, as he crossed the threshold, that dying in a knife fight in the open and under attack, would have been liberating for him, a joyous celebration, on the first night in the clinic when they gave him an injection. He thought that if he had been able to choose or dream about his death at that time, this was the kind of death which he would have chosen or dreamed about.

The role of immortality in time, which can also be integrated into a multiple-layer model of conceptual mapping in this case, has been discussed by a number of scholars in Hispanic studies. One such approach, in line with the information above, can be seen according to the following arguments.[5]

The book which accompanies Dahlmann on his travels, *The Arabian Nights*, plays an important role since it leads him to the "noble" death he desires. He tries to read the book when he rushes up the stairs and has the accident. He tries again on his trip south and when he is in the general store at the end of the story. In *The Arabian Nights*, the main protagonist in the tales, Scheherazade, succeeds in escaping death by recounting various stories. Dahlmann, however, does not escape death, but *the Arabian Nights* leads him to the desired exit in the predicament in which he finds himself.

Furthermore, Borges attempts to show that Dahlmann's time-line in the protagonist's life is one in which time and space defy death. The notion of immortality creeps in due to the rejection of a linear dimension brought about by the intermingling of reality and fantasy. Space and time are doubled by this mixture, and it takes place when Dahlmann leaves the hospital. As a result, his trip to the south is a journey into the past, in which past time is reflected by a different geographical space. The second part of the story is therefore a reverse reflection on the first part: the desire to have a mythical death rather than the grotesque and trivial death in the hospital resulting from sepsis. The doubling effect in the fantasy world is enhanced by Dahlmann being a mirror of the mythical and romantic death of his grandfather.

It has been suggested that the conceptualisation of infinity is reinforced by the use of verb tenses in the story.[6] The succession of events in the first part of the story, the real world of Dahlmann, is mainly recounted in the Spanish preterite form. When the narrative enters the fantasy world of Dahlmann's trip south, the imperfect is often used to describe characteristics of the town which have not changed. In other words, given situations are not finished or without a particular result. At the very end of the story, i.e. the last sentence, the verb tense switches to the present. The use of this tense denotes eternity or a mythical situation. In other words, Dahlmann escapes time, the future no longer exists and linear time is thereby rejected.

11.4 Language-Specific Symbolism in Borges

Syntax in the narrative illustrates an interesting difference in the cross-language structure with regard to the connotations of time. The subtle use of tense to depict personal attitudes towards the conceptualisation of time may often be translated into a language like English. However, as could be seen in the Spanish poetry of Montejo in the preceding chapter, it is not always the case. The preterite (simple past) and present forms fit into equivalent contextual forms, but the imperfect cannot always be used in the same way. One particular verb conjugation is striking with regard to the third person form in the imperfect: the Spanish ending of...*aba(n)* and the English structure *was/were....+ing,* as in *esperaba(n) (was/were waiting).* The following passage illustrates the point with the original Spanish imperfect form in brackets[7:]

> From inside the car, he **searched** (***buscaba***) among the new buildings for the window with grilles, the doorknocker, the archway, the hallway, the cosy patio.

In the main hall of the station, he noticed he still **had** (*faltaban*) thirty minutes. He suddenly remembered that in a coffee shop in Brasil street, (a few yards from Yrigoyen House), there was a huge cat which **let itself be stroked** (*se dejaba acariciar*) by customers, a bit like a disdainful divinity. He went in. The cat **was** (*estaba*) there, asleep. He ordered a cup of coffee, slowly added sugar, tasted it, (he had not had such a pleasure while in the clinic), and thought, while **he was stroking** (*alisaba*) the black fur, that the contact was just an illusion and they **were** (*estaban*) separated by a pane of glass because man lives in chronological time and the magic of an animal in the present, in the eternity of a moment.

In each case, the English equivalent has to be translated by a preterite form, such as *buscaba*/searched, *faltaban*/had, *se dejaba acariciar*/ let itself be stroked, etc. The only exception in this passage is the verbal construction, "while he was stroking", since standard English grammar usually requires the imperfect -*ing* form when another event occurs at the same time in the past. In this case, the event is the action on thinking (i.e. that the contact was just an illusion).

The fact that the Spanish imperfect tense embodies the notion that an event has not come to an end, explains why it lays the foundation for the remark at the end of the passage that the symbol of the cat represents the eternity of a moment. The linear scale of time in human thinking, depicted in the original text as one moment after the next in succession, is rejected by Dahlmann who, like the sleeping cat, seeks eternity in the present moment.

11.5 Fantasy and the Defiance of Death

On the basis of these literary views and this interpretation of the story, it could be argued that traditional conceptualisation of time and space undergoes an additional type of transformation in which linearity is rejected. Although space is intermingled with time, such as the past being represented by the south, the notion of finiteness disappears. This would represent a different form of conceptualisation to the religious notion of the after-life in Dickinson. The movement from the real world of the narrator to a fantasy world is one which rejects finiteness and thereby *defies death*.

A cognitive analysis of symbolic origins in the text would therefore reveal that a multiple conceptual-mapping model may be drawn up in the following way. It appears that death is linked to time in the form of a basic DEATH IS TIME conceptual symbol. A specific extension to this can be seen in the form of a DEATH IS INFINITY mapping.

The multiple mappings involve a primary phase in which Borges projects aspects of his personal biography onto Dahlmann, the main protagonist in the story. A secondary phase implies that Dahlmann creates a fantasy world to escape his predicament of an impending death due to sepsis incurred from his accident. A third cognitive mapping phase implies the symbols used by Borges to defy death by going back to the past. In the case of language structures, the example mentioned above illustrates how a language-specific construction of the imperfect tense in Spanish symbolises the past and how the protagonist wishes to attain it. In addition to language structure, there are other secondary symbols supporting the base DEATH IS INFINITY symbol which are used to depict the past: the station, the coffee-shop which is still there, the cat, even tasting the same brand of coffee which Dahlmann had not drunk for a long time. Later on, other cultural symbols are used such as the gauchos responsible for his escape from an ignoble death and the link to the romantic past of Dahlmann's grandfather. In many ways, it could be suggested that linearity of time is replaced by a cyclic pattern since Dahlmann, via his fantasy world, finally goes back to his past.[8]

How does the aspect of multiple mapping initially projected by the author tie up with the six-tier model proposed in the foregoing discussions? The final chapter will examine the overall process involved in tracing figurative origins.

Notes

1 Borges [1956] (2018: 122): "… of the South, which is perhaps my best story…")
2 Saura (1992): an Argentinian-Spanish production.
3 Op.cit. (2018: 214).
4 idem. Borges (2018: 211).
5 Léglise (2014: 257–268).
6 idem. Léglise (2014: paras. 24–28 – electronic version).
7 Op. cit. Borges (2018: 214).
8 This idea has also been suggested by op.cit. Léglise (2014: para. 2).

12 The Overall Picture

On the basis of the six-tier model of components proposed in the search for origins, i.e. linguistic structures, figurative thought, cultural history, reference, narrative and personal biography, the following pattern may be extrapolated. These components not only represent the projection of a concept from a source to the target domain in a given figurative expression but also all the factors which influence its creation. The links between narrative and personal biography may also involve various forms of mappings related to the real and fantasy worlds of both the protagonist and the author. Within this context, a mapping is perceived in a very wide sense as any transfer of one setting to another, whether it be the projection of an image between semantic fields or a setting between sub-worlds in fiction.

When we read the text of a poem or novel, certain typical linguistic structures can be seen which form a part of the language we use. At this first level, some are conventional and are often used in everyday language. They may be in the form of well-known, single words or structures such as idiomatic phrases. Others can be comprehensible innovations but which may not constitute standard dictionary entries. On the other hand, some innovations may be particularly difficult to interpret, as in Cummings' poetry discussed in chapter 2.

The potential for creating new figurative items may depend on language-specific structures, as in aspects related to morpho-syntax or phonology. Difficulties in translating certain figurative items highlight this specificity. It was seen in the preceding chapter that language-specific structures such as the imperfect tense in Spanish are linked to the symbol of *the South* since they convey the notion of the past.

DOI: 10.4324/9781032130378-12

The symbolic use of the imperfect tense here may not necessarily be used in other languages in the same way as the differentiation between *ser* and *estar* (to be) is used in Montejo's poetry.

If words are traced back further, the second level of figurative thought becomes apparent. Ideas in a narrative are mapped onto underlying figurative constructs. These involve the transfer of images from a source domain to a target concept. The theoretical framework proposed in this study is conceptual metaphor theory. Two main mappings discussed in the literary works here concern the theme of death: the first is the LOVE IS DEATH conceptual metaphor and the second is the related DEATH IS TIME mapping. It appears that, within the six-tier model, the observation of such mappings reveals that not only are stylistic effects enhanced but they can also lead onto the rationale behind the origins of figurative language. Although these particular models of death conceptualisation do not usually represent conventional metaphors in everyday language, they appear to be a common stylistic tool in the history of literary discourse.

Continuing the path for the search into origins, the third level of cultural history, which is integrally tied up with conceptual metaphors, is apparent in a great deal of figurative language. Although some mappings with universal trends exist, which are often based on physiology, many of the more innovative figures of speech in literature have a cultural origin. This may be linked to either a specific culture or to a particular historical period. It was seen in chapter five that Shakespeare's metonyms of "kissing-comfits" and "snow-eryngoes" require cultural knowledge of the time to understand the terms. Cultural information reveals a conceptual metaphor for the former term, such as COMFITS ARE KISSING, which is mapped onto a composite noun in the linguistic metaphor.

At a deeper level of investigation, the fourth feature of reference goes beyond conceptual mappings to what they actually refer to within a contextual dimension. This is known as the referent or referential point. It involves the central person, event or object, which is the subject of the mapping. This may not always be clear in discourse since the reference of a metaphor can change and interpretation is extremely flexible. However, it is not only fundamental to the meaning of a specific figure of speech; an entire symbolic allegory of a novel may be a referential point. In the case of autobiographical trends, the ongoing references in the narrative can give clues as to whether the author is personally involved.

As pointed out in chapter six, these features have been discussed in theories such as mental spaces and discourse worlds. A simple example is the pronoun "I" used in a poem which may often refer to the poet's personal situation. The term proposed here, *hidden reference theory*, and also discussed in chapter six, highlights the difficulty of determining such references. The differences between narrative and autobiography show that, as far as a particular protagonist in fiction is concerned, a symbolic reference *at the textual level* in the narrative may be clear on the basis of context. However, an extended inference to the author may be less so and can therefore represent a hidden referential point. In other words, does a particular symbol refer to the plot alone or ultimately to the author?

At the fifth level of narrative, chapter seven examines different plots in comparative literature which have similar conceptual metaphors. Two relatively complex plots include Harry Haller's life in Hesse's *Steppenwolf* and the love triangle between Pierre, Françoise and Xavier in Beauvoir's novel, *She Came to Stay*. Both narratives involve an over-riding LOVE IS DEATH metaphor at various stages of the plots. In the first example, the metaphor refers to Haller's difficulty in finding a satisfactory love relationship in life. In the second, it is about Françoise's attempt to manage a three-way love relationship in which the presence of one member, Xavière, exerts a destructive force.

Despite the same basic metaphor between the two narratives, its origins are quite different. In *Steppenwolf*, it deals with Haller's psychological make-up. In *She Came to Stay*, the destructive force stems from Beauvoir's interest in existentialist philosophy. In this way, it can be seen that figurative language in a text can often be ultimately traced to the final level of personal experience and biography. There is a great deal of evidence to show that Haller is a mirror of Hermann Hesse and Françoise a mirror of Simone De Beauvoir. Hesse's psychological anxieties are reflected in Haller, and Beauvoir's convictions about Existentialism can be seen in Françoise's behaviour.

This comparison reveals a number of origins in the LOVE IS DEATH metaphor, as adopted by Hesse and Beauvoir in their writing. In this respect, the final level of personal experience in the six-tier model may constitute a complex of multiple mappings in its relationship to narrative structures. One particular dimension of thought, which highlights these variations, concerns the associated DEATH IS TIME conceptual metaphor. This example contrasts real worlds with non-real, or fantasy worlds in both the author's life and a given scenario.

The first observation is that a definition of the real world is not always easy to formulate, even on the basis of scientific facts. The world of astronomy is a case in point. The Ancient Greeks were unaware that Venus is a single planet and it led to two forms of personification of the planet. Today, the notion of time dilation, related to fast-moving objects in outer space, is difficult to conceptualise since the phenomenon does not exist on Earth. It has led to a number of varying real or fantasy worlds in science fiction. Furthermore, a real world may be based on beliefs. A philosophical belief is that every person is responsible for his or acts, as in existentialism. A religious belief is that there is an after-life and that time in a soul's existence is eternal.

The second observation is that, on the basis of actual events which have occurred in the life of an author, the influence of personal experience in writing may be transformed between actual life and a real or fantasy life of a protagonist in a narrative. This may happen in a number of different ways and can form a part of a multiple-mapping complex within personal biography.

One intriguing route is the projection of an author's real world onto one expressed figuratively in the narrative. Distinctions between real and fantasy worlds appear in figurative thought. In the case of Linstead's poem, *The Prospect Behind Us* in chapter 1, it appears that the pantomime world expressed in figurative language actually reflects a real-life predicament. People in the pandemic are subject to an invisible threat in the form of a virus. In Montejo's poem, *Transfigured Time* in chapter 10, it seems that the poet's desire to go back to the past to see his family represents a fantasy world. In this respect, the latter would be a real-to-fantasy mapping. The events do not represent a state of affairs which is actually taking place. Both poems involve events moving backwards and forwards between the past and future, according to the observer's deictic centre. However, the narrative worlds according to reality and fantasy are different.

An even more intricate route is one which involves the use of a third-person configuration. Instead of the author being projected directly onto a first-person identity, a mapping to a third-person protagonist in narrative involves either the latter's real world depicted in the plot or it being depicted in a fantasy world. In other words, the author may project parts of his or her life onto another real world in fiction or onto a fantasy world. The process can lead to a situation in which multiple mappings become apparent.

In Borges' novel, *The South*, it was seen in the previous chapter that the author appears to project his own life onto the protagonist, Dahlmann. In the first part of the story, Dahlmann is actually leading a real life in the protagonist's own eyes. Theoretically, this suggests that Borges has mapped his real world onto another real world. One formulation would therefore be the process of a real world (the life of Borges) being mapped onto a real world (the real life perceived by Dahlmann).

It was also seen that Dahlmann appears to enter his own fantasy world by going south to avoid the dishonourable death of sepsis. If this is the case, Borges first maps his real world onto a real world within a fictional context, as described above. He then changes this mapping half-way through the storyline when Dahlmann travels south. This part of the scenario would then become a change of mapping from a real/real to real/fantasy sub-world. On this basis, it could be argued that the origins of the real/fantasy mapping represent Borges' own nostalgia about the geographical area of his ancestors. This interpretation of mappings could also be an ambiguous one if the real intentions of the author are not known. As mentioned above, Borges leaves this up to the reader.

Whatever the author's real intentions are, multiple possibilities of mappings lead to several basic conceptual metaphors linked to the symbol of time. The DEATH IS TIME mapping encompasses the protagonist's desire to defy death by going back into the past. Extended conceptual metaphors appear, such as DEATH IS INFINITY which stems from the defiance of death. These types of mappings could lead onto others such as the past being associated with a geographical or spatial construct: THE SOUTH IS THE (SENTIMENTAL) PAST. The rationale behind all the symbolic imagery employed in the story is linked to these personal origins. In this way, Borges weaves an intricate network of real and non-real mappings between his own world and the fiction he writes.

The foregoing discussions and analyses suggest that the ultimate origins of much of our figurative language can go back a long way though different levels of conceptual mapping. In literary discourse, at least, it seems that they can very often be linked to the personal experience of an author. The different processes of the theoretical model proposed here may be fused instantaneously or come into play successively as words and thoughts are jotted down, or carefully weighed up, during the writing of a narrative. Without knowing the precise intentions of an author, a great deal about conceptual mappings may be left as unknown territory. There are no doubt many more variations to the basic types illustrated here, and it would appear that a great deal more research is needed on this aspect. However, the different levels of analysis suggested above can provide some solid clues as to the kinds of thoughts in the author's mind which initiate the wealth of figurative language to be found in literary discourse.

References

Bell, Michael (2015). Freud and Lawrence: Thoughts on War and Instinct. *Études lawrenciennes*, 46. https://journals.openedition.org/lawrence/228 [accessed: 27/04/2020].
Bensimon, Paul (1990). Ces métaphores vives ... La traduction des adjectifs composés métaphoriques. *Palimpsestes*, 2: 83–108. 10.4000/palimpsestes.722 [accessed: 20/04/2021].
Bessinger, J.B. Jr. (1977). *A Short Dictionary of Anglo-Saxon Poetry*. Toronto and Buffalo: University of Toronto Press.
Bezuidenhout, Anne L. (2008). Metaphorical singular reference: the role of enriched composition in reference resolution. *The Baltic International Yearbook of Cognition, Logic and Communication*, 3: 1–22.
Booth, Howard J. (1999). 'A dream of life': D. H. Lawrence, utopia and death. *English Studies*, 80(5): 462–478. https://www.tandfonline.com/doi/pdf/10.1080/00138389908599199?needAccess=true [accessed: 27/04/2020].
Borbely, Antal F. (1998). A psychoanalytic concept of metaphor. *International Journal of Psychoanalysis*, 79: 923–936.
Borges, Jorge Luis [1956] (2018). *Ficciones*, 14th edition. Ciudad Autónoma de Buenos Aires: Debolsillo.
Boroditsky, L., Schmidt, L. A., Phillips, W. (2003). Sex, syntax, and semantics. In: Gentner Dedre & Susan Goldin-Meadow (eds.), *Language in Mind. Advances in the Study of Language and Thought*. Cambridge, MA: MIT Press, 61–78.
Boroditsky, Lera (2000). Metaphoric structuring: understanding time through spatial metaphors. *Cognition*, 75: 1–28. https://pcl.sitehost.iu.edu/rgoldsto/courses/concepts/boroditsky2000.pdf [accessed: 12/04/2020].
Bouttier, S. (2013). Adjectives and anti-imperialism in Lawrence's poetry. *Études Lawrenciennes, Language and Languages*, 44: 77–96. https://journals.openedition.org/lawrence/188 [accessed: 02/05/2019].
Bowdle, B., Gentner, D. (2005). The career of metaphor. *Psychological Review*, 112: 193–216.
Brault-Dreux, E. (2013). The "thingness" of the quick. *Etudes Lawrenciennes, Language and Languages*, 44: 23–43. https://journals.openedition.org/lawrence/18 [accessed: 02/05/2019].

Brockmeier, J. (1994). Translating temporality. Narrative schemes and cultural meanings of time. Public lecture presented at Collegiums in Budapest, Institute for Advanced Study. ISSN 1217-5811 ISBN 963 8463 104.
Brown, Meg L., Kari B. McBride (2005). *Women's Roles in the Renaissance*. Westport, CT: Greenwood Press.
Cabré, M-T. (1992 [1998]). *La terminologie. Théorie, méthode et applications*. Ottawa and Paris: Les presses de l'Université d'Ottawa & Armand Colin.
Cabré, M-T. (2004). Introduccio: La importancia de la neologia per al desenvolupament sostenible de la llengua catalana, Observatori de neologia, Institut Universari de Linguistica Aplicada, Universitat Pompeu Fabra, Llengua catalana i neologia, Meteora, Barcelone, 17–45.
Cazé, A. (2007). E. E. Cummings: (dé)composition d'adjectifs, inventivité linguistique et traduction. *Palimpsestes*, 19: 135–164.
Chevalier, Jean, Gheerbrant, Alain (1969). *Dictionnaire des Symboles. Mythes, Rêves, Coutûmes, Gestes, Formes, Figures, Couleurs, Nombres*. Paris: Editions Robert Laffont, S.A. & Editions Jupiter.
Chickering, Howell D. (1977). *Beowulf. A Dual-Language Edition*. New York: Anchor Books.
Chomsky, Noam (1957). *Syntactic Structures*. The Hague/Paris: Mouton.
The Concise Oxford Dictionary of Current English. (1990). Oxford: Clarendon Press.
Cummings, E. E. (1972). *Complete Poems 1913–1962*. San Diego: Harcourt Trade Publishers.
Daiches, David (1960). *The Novel and the Modern World*. Cambridge: Cambridge University Press.
De Beauvoir, Simone (1943). *L'Invitée*. Paris: Editions Gallimard. English translation: *She Came to Stay* (1990). London and New York: Norton & Company.
De Saussure, Ferdinand (1916). *Cours de linguistique générale*. Lausanne, Paris: Payot.
Dickinson, Emily. [1890] (1998). In: Ralph W. Franklin (ed.), *The Poems of Emily Dickinson*. Cambridge, MA: The Belknap Press of Harvard University Press.
Dickinson, Emily [1890] (2003). In: Nina Baym (ed.), *Poems. The Norton Anthology of American Literature*, 6th edition. New York: W. W. Norton.
Dion, R., Regard, F. (eds.) (2013). *Les Nouvelles écritures biographiques – La Biographie d'écrivain dans ses reformulations contemporaines*. Lyon: ENS Editions. https://books.openedition.org/enseditions/4499 [accessed: 02/05/2019].
Dor, J. (2003). The wife of Bath's "wandrynge by the weye" and conduct literature for women. In: W. Harding (ed.), *Drama, Narrative and Poetry in the Canterbury Tales*. Toulouse: Presses Universitaires du Mirail, 139–155.
Dorst, Aletta G. (2019). Translating metaphorical mind style: machinery and ice metaphors in Ken Kesey's *One Flew over the Cuckoo's Nest*. *Perspectives – Studies in Translation Theory and Practice*, 27(6): 875–889.

Doubrovsky, Serge (1977). *Le fils*. Collection Folio, Paris: Gallimard.
Ellis, David (ed.) (1998). *D. H. Lawrence: dying game 1922–1930*. Cambridge: Cambridge University Press.
Fauconnier, Gilles (1994). *Mental Spaces*. Cambridge: Cambridge University Press.
Fauconnier, Gilles (1997). *Mappings in Thought and Language*. Cambridge: Cambridge University Press.
Fauconnier, Gilles, Turner, Mark (2003). Conceptual blending, form and meaning. *Recherches en Communication*, 19. https://www.researchgate.net/publication/45359086_Conceptual_Blending_Form_and_Meaning [accessed: 20/04/2021].
Fedosova, Tatyana (2015). Reflection of time in postmodern literature. *Athens Journal of Philology*, 2: 77–88. 10.30958/ajp.2-2-1 [accessed: 10/9/2020].
Fludernik, Monika (ed.) (2011). *Beyond Cognitive Metaphor Theory: Perspectives on Literary Metaphor*. New York: Routledge.
Fowler, H. W., Fowler, F. G. (1990). *The Concise Oxford Dictionary of Current English*. Oxford: Clarendon Press.
Fowler, R. (1977). *Linguistics and the Novel*. London: Methuen.
Frege, Gottlob (1892). Über Sinn und Bedeutung, *Zeitschrift für Philosophie und philosophische Kritik*, Vol. 100, 25–50. Leipzig.
Freud, Sigmund [1920] 1990. In: James Strachey (ed.), *Beyond the Pleasure Principle*. Norton, MA: Norton Library.
Friedman, Alan W. (2000). *D. H. Lawrence: pleasure and death. Studies in the Novel*, Vol. 32, N° 32, N° 2, Death in the Novel. Baltimore: The John Hopkins University Press, 207–228.
Gibbs, R. W. (1994). *The Poetics of Mind. Figurative Thought, Language and Understanding*. New York: Cambridge University Press.
Girardin, Saint-Marc (1845). *Cours de Littérature Dramatique*. Vol. 1. Paris. http://www.shakespeare-online.com/plays/romeoandjuliet/romeotastedeath.html [accessed: 20/04/2021].
Goatly, A. (2007). *Washing the Brain: Metaphor and Hidden Ideology*. Amsterdam/Philadelphia: John Benjamins.
Gouirand-Rousselon, J. (2002). *L'Arc-en-ciel*. Paris: Éditions Autrement.
Growse, Nicholas (2012). Lawrence and the ideology of emotion. *Etudes Lawrenciennes*, 43: 237–255. https://journals.openedition.org/lawrence/103 [accessed: 28/04/2020].
Günther, G. (1964). *Der Regenbogen*. Hamburg: Rowohlt Taschenbuch.
Harris, R. (1976). Comprehension of metaphor: a test of a two-stage processing model. *Bulletin of the Psychonomics Society*, 8: 321–324.
Hausman, Carl R. (1983). Metaphors, referents and individuality. *The Journal of Aesthetics and Art Criticism*, 42(2): 181–195. Wiley. 10.2307/430662 [accessed: 20/04/2021].
Hesse, Hermann (1927). *Steppenwolf*. Berlin: Fischer Verlag. First English translation: Steppenwolf. London: Secker (1929).

Hieatt, A., Hieatt, C. (1976). *Chaucer. Canterbury Tales.* New York: Bantam.
Hoad, T. F. (1987). *The Concise Oxford Dictionary of English Etymology.* Oxford: Clarendon Press.
Howard, Donald R. (1960). The conclusion of the marriage group: chaucer and the human condition. *Modern Philology*, 57(4): 223–232.
Jenny, Laurent (2003). *Méthodes et problèmes. L'autofiction.* https://www.unige.ch/lettres/framo/enseignements/methodes/autofiction/afintegr.html [accessed: 14/2/2020].
Kenney, E. J. (2008). Introduction. In: *Ovid. Metamorphoses.* Oxford World Classics. Oxford: Oxford University Press.
Kesey, K. (1962). *One Flew Over the Cuckoo's Nest.* Groningen: Wolters-Noordhoff.
Kittay, E. F. (1987). *Metaphor: Its Cognitive Force and Linguistic Structure.* Oxford: Clarendon.
Kleiber, G. (1984). Dénomination et relations dénominatives. *Langages*, 76: 77–94. 10.3406/lgge.1984.1496 [accessed: 12/06/2020].
Kleiber, G. (1997). Sens, référence et existence: que faire de l'extralinguistique? *Langages*, 127: 9–37. https://www.persee.fr/doc/lgge_0458-726x_1997_num_31_127_2123 [accessed: 12/06/2020].
Kövecses, Zoltán (1988). *The Language of Love.* London and Toronto: Associated University Presses.
Kövecses, Zoltán (2000). *Metaphor and Emotion: Language, Culture and Body in Human Feeling.* Cambridge: Cambridge University Press.
Kövecses, Zoltán (2005). *Metaphor in Culture. Universality and Variation.* Cambridge: Cambridge University Press.
Kövecses, Zoltán (2006). *Language, Mind and Culture.* Oxford: Oxford University Press.
Kövecses, Zoltán (2015). *Where Metaphors Come From. Reconsidering Context in Metaphor.* Oxford: Oxford University Press.
Kripke, Saul A. (1980). *Naming and Necessity.* Cambridge: Harvard University Press.
Lakoff, George (1987). *Women, Fire and Dangerous Things.* Chicago: University of Chicago Press.
Lakoff, George (1991). Cognitive versus generative linguistics: how commitments influence results. *Language and communication*, 11(1/2): 53–62.
Lakoff, George, Johnson, Mark (1980). *Metaphors We Live By.* Chicago: University of Chicago Press.
Lakoff, George, Turner, Mark (1989). *More Than Cool Reason. A Field Guide to Poetic Metaphor.* Chicago: University of Chicago Press.
Lawrence, D. H. (1915). *The Rainbow.* London: Methuen & Co.
Lawrence, D. H. (1920). *Women in Love.* New York: Thomas Seltzer.
Lawrence, D. H. (1922). *Fanny and Annie. England, My England.* New York: Thomas Seltzer.
Lawrence, D. H. (1923). *Birds, Beasts and Flowers.* London: Martin Secker.

References

Léglise, Florence (2014). Espace, temps et mort dans El Sur de Jorge Luis Borges: construction spéculaire, labyrinthe de spéculations. *La realidad y el deseo*, OpenEdition Books. Lyon: ENS Editions, 257–268. https://books.openedition.org/enseditions/1611 [accessed: 03/06/2020].

Linstead, Stephen (ed.) (2020). Viral verses. Art in exceptional times. https://www.viralverses.com/ [accessed: 08/04/2021].

Locke, John [1689] (1988). *An Essay Concerning Human Understanding*. Oxford: Oxford University Press.

Lukavská, Eva (1977). *L'Invitée* de Simone De Beauvoir. *Etudes Romanes de Brno*, Vol. IX, 51–64. https://digilib.phil.muni.cz/bitstream/handle/11222.digilib/113574/1_EtudesRomanesDeBrno_09-1977-1_5.pdf?sequence=1 [accessed: 01/05/2020].

Maas, David (2003). Reflections on self-reflexiveness in literature. *E.T.C.: A Review of General Semantics*. https://www.thefreelibrary.com/Reflections+on+self-reflexiveness+in+literature.-a0111011254 [accessed: 22/05/2020].

Mainguenaud, D. (2002), Linguistique et littérature: le tournant discursif. *Vox Poetica*. http://www.vox-poetica.org/t/articles/maingueneau.html [accessed: 02/05/2019].

Marnat, Marcel (1966). *D. H. Lawrence. Classiques du XXe siècle*. Paris: Editions Universitaires.

Mayakovsky, Vladimir (1975). *Poemy i stikhotvorenia* (Poems and Verses). Moscow: Khudozhestvennaya Literatura.

McNamara, Daniele, Magliano, Joe (2009). Toward a comprehensive model of comprehension. In: B. Ross (ed.), *The Psychology of Learning and Motivation – Advances in Research and Theory*, 51: 297–384.

Means, Philip Ainsworth [1931] (1973). *Ancient Civilisations of the Andes*. New York: Gordian Press.

Mejri, S., Sablayrolles, J.-F. (2011). Présentation: Néologie, nouveaux modèles théoriques et NTIC. *Langages*, 183, 3–9. https://www.cairn.info/revue-langages-2011-3-page-3.htm [accessed: 02/05/2019].

Messud, Claire (2018). *The Burning Girl*. London and New York: Norton & Company.

Moi, Toril (1994). *Simone de Beauvoir: The Making of an Intellectual Woman*. Oxford (UK) and Cambridge (USA): Blackwell. French translation by Guillemette Belleteste (1995): *Simone de Beauvoir: Conflits d'une intellectuelle*. Paris, New York, Amsterdam: Diderot Editeur, Arts et Sciences.

Monte, Michèle (2020). Stabilité et instabilité du sens dans les énoncés métaphoriques en poésie. In: E. Hilgert, S. Palma, G. Kleiber, P. Frath, R. Daval (dir.), *Lexique et référence «Res per Nomen 7»*, 2020. Reims: EPURE, 305–320.

Montejo, Eugenio (1996). *El taller blanco y otros ensayos*. Mexico: Universidad Autónoma Metropolitana.

Montejo, Eugenio (2001). *Tiempo transfigurado*. Valencia: Ediciones Poesía. English translation: Peter Boyle, *Transfigured Time*.

Moore, Kevin (2006). Space-to-time mappings and temporal concepts. *Cognitive Linguistics*, 17: 199–244.
Nikitina, Svetlana (2009). Innovation and multimedia in the poetry of Cummings and Mayakovsky. CLCWeb. *Comparative Literature and Culture*, 11(4). 10.7771/1481-4374.1557 [accessed: 19/04/2021].
Niven, A. (1978). *D. H. Lawrence. The Novels.* Cambridge: Cambridge University Press.
Noguerol, Francisca (2011). Eugenio Montejo: terredad y altura. In: Carmen Ruiz Barrionuevo et al. (eds.), *Voces y escrituras de Venezuela*. Caracas: Centro Nacional del Libro, CENAL, 299–306. https://www.researchgate.net/publication/281233513_Eugenio_Montejo_terredad_y_altura [accessed: 11/02/2020].
Nunberg, Geoffrey (2006). *How Conservatives Turned Liberalism into a Tax-Raising, Latte-drinking, Sushi-eating, Volvo-driving, New-York Times-Reading, Body-Piercing, Hollywood-Loving, Left-Wing Freak Show.* New York: Public Affairs.
Nyckees V. (2007). La cognition humaine saisie par le langage: de la sémantique cognitive au médiationnisme, *Corela*, HS 6. https://journals.openedition.org/corela/1543] [accessed: 02/05/2019].
Pillière, Linda (2013). Mind style: deviance from the norm? *Études de stylistique anglaise* 4, *Style in Fiction Today.* Open Edition Journals. https://journals.openedition.org/esa/1448 [accessed: 23/04/2020].
Plaza, Arturo Gutiérrez (2007). Un itinerario de oblicuas huellas. *Hispanic Poetry Review*, 6(2): 13–50. https://www.academia.edu/39892890/EUGENIO_MONTEJO_UN_ITINERARIO_DE_OBLICUAS_HUELLAS [accessed: 13/02/2020].
Prandi, Michele (2017). *Conceptual Conflicts in Metaphors and Figurative Language.* New York and London: Routledge Studies in Linguistics.
Proust, Marcel [1919]. *A la Recherche du Temps Perdu.* Paris: Gallimard. English translation: William C. Carter (ed.), In: *Search of Lost Time.* New Haven: Yale University Press (2013).
Putnam, Hilary (1981). *Reason, Truth, and History.* Cambridge: Cambridge University Press.
Rabatel, A. (2014). Quelques remarques sur la théorie argumentative de la polyphonie. *Arena romanistica*, 14: 204–222.
Rabatel, A. (2015). Du sujet, des œuvres et de l'interprétation. In: C. Masseron, J-M. Privat, Y. Reuter (eds.), *Littérature, linguistique et didactique du français. Les travaux Pratiques d'André Petitjean.* Villeneuve d'Ascq: Presses universitaires du Septentrion, 97–105.
Radden, Günther (2003). The metaphor TIME AS SPACE across languages. *Zeitschrift für Interkulturellen Fremdsprachenunterricht*, 8(2/3): 1–4.
Richards, I. (1965). *The Philosophy of Rhetoric.* Oxford: Oxford University Press.
Ricoeur, Paul ([1975] 1978). *La métaphore vive.* Paris: Editions du Seuil. English translation: *The Rule of Metaphor: Multi-Disciplinary Studies in the Creation of Meaning in Language.* Toronto: University of Toronto Press.

Roberts, Nicholas (2009). *Poetry and Loss: The Work of Eugenio Montejo*. Woodbridge: Tamesis Books.
Rosch, E. (1975). Cognitive representations of semantic categories. *Journal of Experimental Psychology*, 104(3): 192–233.
Russel, Karen (2014). *Vampires in the Lemon Grove*. NewYork: Vintage Contemporaries.
Sartre, Jean-Paul (1946). *L'existentialisme est un humanisme*. Paris: Gallimard.
Semino, E., Swindlehurst, K. (1996). Metaphor and mind style in Ken Kesey's *One Flew over the Cuckoo's Nest*. *Style*, 30(1): 143–166.
Semino, Elena (2007). *Mind Style Twenty-Five Years On. Style. Vol. 41, N° 2, Style in Fiction*. University Park, PA: Penn State University Press, 153–172.
Shipley, Joseph T. (1984). *The Origins of English Words. A Discursive Dictionary of Indo-European Roots*. Baltimore: John Hopkins University Press.
Sinha, Chris, Sinha, Vera da Silva, Zinken, Jörg, Sampaio, Wany (2011). When time is not space: the social and linguistic construction of time intervals and temporal event relations in an Amazonian culture. *Language and Cognition*, 3(1): 137–169.
Skinner, B. F. (1938). *The Behavior of Organisms*. New York: Appleton-Century-Crofts.
Smith, M., Pollio, H., Pitts, M. (1981). Metaphor as intellectual history: conceptual categories underlying figurative usage in American English from 1675 to 1975. *Linguistics*, 19: 911–935.
Spilka, Mark (ed.) (1963). *D.H.Lawrence: A Collection of Critical Essays*. New York: Prentice-Hall.
Steen, Gerd (2017). Deliberate metaphor theory: basic assumptions, main tenets, urgent issues. *Intercultural Pragmatics*, 14(1): 1–24.
Stekel, Wilhelm (1911). *Die Sprache des Traumes. Eine Darstellung der Symbolik und Deutung des Traumes in ihren Beziehungen zur kranken und gesunden Seele*. Wiesbaden: Wiesbaden Verlag.
Stockwell, Peter (2002). *Cognitive Poetics: An Introduction*. New York and Abingdon: Routledge.
Tissari, Heli (2003). LOVEscapes. Changes in prototypical senses and cognitive metaphors since 1500. In: Matti Rissanen, Juhani Härmä, Jarmo Korhonen (eds.), *Mémoires de la Société Néophilologique de Helsinki*. LXII: Helsinki.
Trim, Richard (2007). *Metaphor Networks. The Comparative Evolution of Figurative Language*. Basingstoke: Palgrave Macmillan.
Trim, Richard (2010). Conceptual networking theory in metaphor evolution: diachronic variation in models of love. In: K. Allan, H. Tessari (eds.), *Historical Cognitive Linguistics*. Berlin: Mouton de Gruyter, 223–260.
Trim, Richard (2011). *Metaphor and the Historical Evolution of Conceptual Mapping*. Basingstoke: Palgrave Macmillan.
Trim, Richard (2015). La traduction des modaux dans *Pride and Prejudice*: approche diachronique (1822–2011). In: A. Joly, D. O'Kelly (eds.), *Modalités*

et modes de discours. Interpréter et traduire. Modèles Linguistiques. Toulon: Editions des Dauphins, Toulon, Vol. 71, 93–106.

Trim, Richard (2018a). L'influence de la morphologie sur l'interprétation des images doubles au sein des métaphores littéraires. Une approche contrastive. In: G. Achard-Bayle, M. Guérin, G. Kleiber, M. Krylyschin (eds.), *Les sciences du langage et la question de l'interprétation (aujourd'hui)*. Limoges: Editions Lambert-Lucas, 155–170.

Trim, Richard (2018b). L'impact de la morpho-syntaxe dans les processus de métaphorisation contrastive entre langues romanes et germaniques. *Neophilologica*, 30. Katowice: Wydawnictwo Uniwersytetu Śląskiego, 328–339.

Trim, Richard (2019). Le conflit et les origines de la métaphore. In: M. Fasciolo, F. Neveu (eds.), *Le conflit conceptuel: De la grammaire aux métaphores*, Langue Française, n° 204 (4/2019). Paris: Armand Colin, 37–51.

Trim, Richard (2021a). Networking at the interface between conceptual and linguistic metaphor in comparative literary texts. In: G. Zocco (ed.), *The Rhetoric of Topics and Forms*. Berlin: Walter de Gruyter, 49–60.

Trim, Richard (2021b). Poetic symbols of time limits: individual and standard cognitive models. *International Association for Semiotic Studies*, 6: 17–28. https://iass-ais.org/proceedings2019/Proceedings_IASS_2019_tomo_6.pdf [accessed: 20/04/2021].

Vukanović, Marija Brala, Lovorka Gruić, Grmuša (2009). *Space and Time in Language and Literature*. Newcastle-upon-Tyne: Cambridge Scholars Publishing.

Warren, Beatrice (2002). An alternative account of the interpretation of referential metonymy and metaphor. In: Dirven René, Ralf Pörings (eds.), *Metaphor and Metonymy in Comparison and Contrast, Cognitive Linguistics Research 20*. Berlin and New York: Mouton de Gruyter, 113–130.

Welsh, Irvine (1991). *Ecstasy. Three Tales of Chemical Romance*. London: Vintage Books.

Whorf, Benjamin (1956). *Language, Thought and Reality*. Cambridge, MA: MIT Press.

Wimsatt, W. K., Monroe, C. B. (1946). The intentional fallacy. *The Sewanee Review*, 54(3): 468–488.

Wimsatt, W. K., Monroe, C. B. (1949). The affective fallacy. *The Sewanee Review*, 57(1): 31–55.

Wlosok, A. (1975). Amor and cupid. *Harvard Studies in Classical Philology*, 79: 165–179.

Zeller, Bernhard (1963). *Hermann Hesse in Selbstzeugnissen und Bilddokumenten*. Hamburg: Rowohlt Taschenbuch Verlag.

Zharikov, S., Gentner, D. (2002). Why do metaphors seem deeper than similes? In: W.D. Gray, C. D. Schunn (eds.), *Proceedings of the Twenty-fourth Annual Conference of the Cognitive Society*. Fairfax: George Mason University, 976–981.

Zwaan, Rolf A., Radvansky, Gabriel A. (1998). Situation models in language comprehension. *Psychological Bulletin*, 123(2): 162–185.

Glossary of Linguistic Terms

Agglutinative language: single words in the language tend to be made up of many morphemes.
Analytical language: many prepositions are used in the language rather than words combining a large number of morphemes.
Calque: a copy or imitation of a word.
Cognate language: one language being etymologically related to another.
Collocations: the way in which words and their meanings normally fit together in standard language.
Conceptual blending: a theory which suggests that different scenarios are mixed together subconsciously in a process that is assumed to be very common in everyday thought and language.
Conceptual metaphor: a figurative comparison in which one conceptual domain is understood in terms of another; e.g. LOVE IS HEAT.
Deictic perception: the process in conceptualisation which is based on the observer's viewpoint.
Diachronic/synchronic: the diachronic dimension involves patterns through time; synchronic involves the same point in time.
Discourse worlds: imaginary scenarios in discourse designed to help the reader understand a narrative.
Extra-linguistic: not directly related to the language structure.
Lexeme: a single root word to which morphemes are added; e.g. "view" is the lexeme of "viewed".
Linguistic metaphor: a metaphor in a text, e.g. "ex-flame", as opposed to its corresponding conceptual metaphor LOVE IS HEAT.

Linguistic relativity:	the extent to which language structure has an impact on thought.
Metonymy:	in contrast to a metaphor, a metonym involves a thing or concept which is referred to by the name of something closely associated with it, e.g. *The White House* for the American administration.
Morpheme:	a feature in a word comprising one unit of meaning.
Morphological derivation:	the ways in which morphemes are added to a word.
Morpho-syntax:	the combination of linguistic features in a word (morphology), such as prefixes and suffixes, and the way in which the word is integrated into a phrase or sentence (syntax).
Neologism:	a newly created word which has not usually been fully accepted in the standard language.
Phonology:	the structure of sounds.
Polysemy:	multiple meanings in a word.
Postpositioning:	placing one linguistic feature after another in a phrase.

Index

acronyms 8–9
affective fallacy 77
Aristotle 34
autofiction 78

behaviourism 32
belief: religious 94; systems 57
biographies 75–88; autobiographies 77; "distortion" 76; individual 79
blends 36; conceptual 56
Boccaccio, G. 44
Borges, J. L. 107–114

calques 27
Chaucer, G. 44
cognates 23
collocations 26
composite/compound structures 13–16; innovation 17; inversion 15; word order 25–26
conceptualisation: ego-centred/non-ego-centred 90; global models 1; individual 33; levels 61; multicultural 91–92; multiple mapping 75, 107–114; prototype 32; time and space 90–92
conflictual paradigms 38
contextual information 63
creativity: figurative 11, 21; individual 13; linguistic 19; processes 63
cross-cultural factors 13
cross-language factors 19
cultural history 43–53
Cummings E.E 17, 20–21

Dante 5
De Beauvoir, S. 68, 82–84

deixis 60, 90
De Saussure, F. 55
diachronic processes 25; conceptual networking 43; salience 45
Dickinson, E. 94–97
discourse worlds 57–58; fictional 57; possible 57; real 89–97; real versus fantasy/non-real 60, 86–87, 106; worldly knowledge 60
domains: source 1, 4; target 1, 4
dynamic processes 62

Early Modern English 51
empiricism 31
epithets 62
etymology 17
existentialism 68, 84
experience: background to personal experience 16; personal 2, 4

figurative thought 30
figures of speech: conventional 13; innovative 15
fixed expressions 17
formal logic 57
Frege, G. 60
Freud, S. 34, 72–73, 81, 84–86

Hesse, H. 70, 84–86

idioms 33
idiosyncrasy 13, 15–16
images: double and multiple 16; single versus multiple 36
intentional fallacy 77
interpretation 13, 17, 55

Kant, I. 31
Keats, J. 57

language: agglutinative 20; analytical 20; components 19; everyday *versus* literary 37; Indo-European 90; language-specific expressions 8; structural distance 21–22; structures 7–9, 11, 13
Lawrence, D. H. 11, 13–15, 66–68, 79–82
lexis: analysis 17; lexemes 18, 21
linguistic relativity 19
linguistics: cognitive 4, 9; contrastive 29; historical 17
Locke, J. 31

mapping: conceptual 1–2, 8, 53; figurative 7; universal 4–5
mediationism 40
mental spaces 56
mental transfer 1
Messud, C. 76
metaphors: anomaly view 34; cognitive 1, 34–35; comparison theory 34; conceptual 1, 4, 7, 9, 35, 37, 44; ideologies 45; innovative 44; interactionist view 34; linguistic 7, 35, 66; living *versus* conventional 39; metaphorisation 17; salience 44; time-specific 50
metonymy 13; Shakespeare 51
mind style 36–37; relation to author 58
Montejo, E. 99–106
morphology: derivation 14, 17; innovative 22–23; language-specific 103; morphemes 20–21; structures 17
morpho-syntax 13, 16

narrative 56–57, 63, 65–66
nativism 31
neologisms 16–18, 25
New Criticism 78
nominalism 55

Old English 17, 47

origins: figurative words 46
orthography 17

personification 4, 12, 48
phonetics 13
phraseology 13
Plath, S. 33
Plato 31
poetic licence 9, 17
polysemy 24, 46, 56
psychology: bipolarity 74; cognitive 31, 62; personal 70

reality: limits 100; transformation 99–106
reference 9, 55–63; extra-linguistic 55–56; hidden reference theory 61; literal 62; philosophical 60; textual 61, 65–66

Sartre, P. 70
science fiction 2
self-reflexiveness 94–95
semantics 13, 27; change 51; complex 17; extension and loss 46; pejoration 23; referential 55; variational 16
semiotics 105
Shakespeare, W. 47–52
signs: images 101; linguistic 46
similes 12, 18, 24, 36
spirituality 101, 104
style: effects 8, 18; tools 16
symbols 4–5, 7–8, 12–13, 16, 27; Borges 107–108; cross-cultural 31; D. H. Lawrence 79; language-specific 112–113; metaphoric 35; Montejo 101–103; Shakespearean 51
synonymy 46
syntax: change 25; structures 25

textual features 61–63
translation 20, 24–25
truth values 57, 60

universals 13, 43, 57

For Product Safety Concerns and Information please contact our EU representative GPSR@taylorandfrancis.com
Taylor & Francis Verlag GmbH, Kaufingerstraße 24, 80331 München, Germany

www.ingramcontent.com/pod-product-compliance
Lightning Source LLC
Chambersburg PA
CBHW051751230426
43670CB00012B/2236